LETTERS
FOR ALL OCCASIONS

*the text of this book is printed
on 100% recycled paper*

About the Author

The late ALFRED STUART MYERS was an experienced writer and editor, formerly head of the English Department at Idaho Industrial Institute and instructor in English at Maryville College. He contributed numerous articles to *Advertising and Selling, Industrial Management, Printer's Ink, The Writer,* and other national journals. During World War II he was in charge of correspondence in one of the largest government branches of the Office of Dependency Benefits. For many years he served as a free-lance editor for leading book publishers and edited notable works in advertising, business management, economics, engineering, history, medicine and sociology.

LETTERS

FOR ALL OCCASIONS

ALFRED STUART MYERS

BARNES & NOBLE BOOKS

A DIVISION OF HARPER & ROW, PUBLISHERS

New York, Evanston, San Francisco, London

Manufactured in the United States of America

Table of Contents

Foreword

Foreword

PERHAPS THE best way to emphasize, right at the start, the importance of effective letter writing is to ask you, the reader: How many times have you received a letter that has fallen short of its goal—whatever that goal may have been? Probably more times than you can remember. It may have been a business letter, with the definite purpose of selling an idea or a product. It may have been one of the many types of social letters: a personal invitation; an acceptance or a regret; a letter of congratulations or greetings; a note accompanying a gift or thanking you for one; a letter of introduction; or, one of the most difficult of all to write, a note of condolence.

Whatever the case, you have often been left with the impression that the letter just did not "have what it takes." Perhaps you did not analyze, or even consciously realize, exactly why you failed to react favorably. Still, the unfavorable impression was there. It may have been the result of the physical make-up of the letter; or of the words used to express an idea; or of the general tone and spirit, a factor subtle and difficult to pin down, but none the less real and important. Perhaps all these factors were involved to some extent. At any rate, when you receive such a communication, you may wonder, Do I write letters like that? Do my letters really say what I mean them to say? Is the impression actually what I want it to be? Such self-questioning is good for the soul—and for your future letter writing. A bad example is sometimes a good example, to state a paradox.

In other words, it sometimes pays to analyze a poorly written letter, when you get one, and to discover its real failings—then to be sure to avoid them in your own letter writing.

As Shakespeare said, "The apparel oft proclaims the man." A similar statement could be made, with equal truth, about the letters that a person writes. Whether it be a social letter, a business letter, or merely a letter from friend to friend, there is in that correspondence something that "proclaims the man." That is why it is so important to make your correspondence speak favorably for you. Certainly you would not go to a social affair carelessly dressed and, among the guests, express yourself in a slovenly manner. You would not make a business call wearing inappropriate clothes or engage in an interview without careful consideration of the good impression you want to make.

So, with letters, it is necessary to create an effective, favorable impression, for whatever purpose a particular letter may be written. To that end, there are certain fundamental principles to be applied. They are simple, but, at all times, they should be strictly observed.

The purpose here is to explain these fundamental principles in straightforward, nontechnical fashion and with examples that will illustrate them and will show how to impart that "spirit" behind the good letter, mentioned earlier. This book is intended to provide a simple, practical guide for the reader who wishes to master the art of effective social and business correspondence.

Part One

FORM IN SOCIAL AND
BUSINESS LETTERS

1

Form in Social Letters

JUST AS a person's clothes and general appearance create a first impression that is likely to be lasting, so the paper and envelope used in correspondence produce an initial effect, favorable or unfavorable, that carries over into the letter itself, for good or ill. That is why these are the very first things to be considered. Obvious, perhaps, but it is surprising how many people are careless in this respect and therefore forfeit an important advantage they might have gained at the start.

We shall not dwell on these factors, since any good stationer can give dependable advice on the subject, but a few remarks may be helpful.

PAPER AND PAGING

Paper. To carry on the parallel of a person's clothes, the letter paper should be neither too plain nor too ornate. Paper with ruled lines gives an impression of cheapness or of immaturity. Some tactless correspondents use paper with bright colors, gilt edges, or large, brilliant monograms, and sometimes even paper cut in an unusual shape. All this can be summed up in two words, "poor taste," which cover a multitude of sins. Such practices attract attention, but not the right kind.

White paper is correct for either men or women. You cannot go wrong with that. Women may also use a delicately tinted paper, and it may or may not carry the address or a dignified monogram. Men may prefer gray paper to white, and in either case it may or may not carry an address.

Neatness of appearance is enhanced by even margins, at both left and right—a slight margin on the right, a little broader one on the left. The letter should be neatly folded so that the edges, top and bottom, meet evenly, and so that the first page faces the person who opens the envelope.

Paging.   The sequence of pages in a letter or a note is worthy of consideration. It is a matter in which there is considerable variety. Here are some of the acceptable procedures with a two-sheet, four-page communication:

1. Write on pages one and three, up and down, and on pages two and four sidewise.

2. Write on pages one and four, up and down, and on pages two and three (the inside pages) sidewise, using them as one large page.

3. Write on all four pages, up and down, in regular sequence—one, two, three, four. This is perhaps best for the reader; he can then find and read the pages of your letter as he would those of a book, easily and quickly.

A three-page letter may be written on pages one and three, up and down, and on page two sidewise; or it may be written on pages one, two, and three, up and down.

A two-page note may be written on pages one and four, up and down, with the two inside pages left blank; or it may be written on pages one and three, up and down.

Whichever of these procedures you use, number your pages. It is a helpful courtesy to your reader and saves him time and exasperation, especially if your letter is a long one.

THE ENVELOPE

Clear information and proper form on an envelope are important both to the post office and to the receiver of your letter.

Correct Title.   Address people by their customary signatures—the ones they use on checks and in business letters. The title *Mr., Mrs.,* or *Miss* should be used unless the individual has some special rank, in which case use that.

Doctor and *Reverend* may be abbreviated, but not in very formal correspondence. The following forms are correct.

FOR A MINISTER: *Reverend* (or *Rev.*) John C. Fleming. If he has the degree of Doctor of Divinity, he may be addressed in one of three ways: *Dr. John C. Fleming; Rev. Dr. John C. Fleming;* or *Rev. John C. Fleming, D.D.*

FOR A PRIEST: *Rev. Father John E. Finnegan; The Reverend John E. Finnegan;* or *The Reverend Father Finnegan.*

FOR A RABBI: either *Rabbi Elihu Meyer* or *Rev. Elihu Meyer.*

FOR A DOCTOR: *Dr. Henry M. Atley,* but never place *M.D.* after this. In correspondence other than social, *Henry M. Atley, M.D.* is allowable, but *Dr.* and *M.D.* are never to be used together.

FOR A PROFESSOR: *Professor William D. Harvey.* If the addressee has the degree of Doctor of Philosophy, the proper form is *Dr. William D. Harvey.*

FOR A VERY YOUNG GIRL: *Miss,* just as you would address her older unmarried sister; use *Master* for a very young boy.

The examples given above represent some of the most common titles you will be called upon to use.

Names of City and State. The name of a city should never be abbreviated. It is perfectly allowable to abbreviate the name of a state, if it is a long one, except in formal correspondence. If the name of a state consists of two words very commonly known, it is permissible to use only the initial letters: *R. I., N. Y., N. H., N. J.*

Indented and Block Forms. In social correspondence, the envelope is sometimes addressed in indented form, with punctuation either (*a*) open or (*b*) closed.

> (*a*) Mr. John Blank
>   105 Fifth Avenue
>   New York, N. Y. 10003
>   or
> (*b*) Mr. John Blank,
>   105 Fifth Avenue,
>   New York, N. Y. 10003

As you will notice, the open punctuation omits commas at the end of the lines; the closed punctuation contains the commas. There are two other forms of address: (*a*) block

> (*a*)   Mr. John Blank
>   105 Fifth Avenue
>   New York, N. Y. 10003
>   or
> (*b*)   Mr. John Blank,
>   105 Fifth Avenue,
>   New York, N. Y. 10003

Note that, whichever form you select, indented or block, you must use it both for the envelope and for the inside heading of the letter.

Return Address. Be sure to place a return address on your envelope, for use in case your letter goes astray or the addressee has moved. Postal authorities advise that the sender's address be placed in the upper left-hand corner of the envelope, on the same side as the address. (In social correspondence, however, the return address is often placed on the back flap of the envelope.) Such special notations as "Please forward" or "Personal" may be written on the front of the envelope in the lower, left-hand corner. The following form is correct:

```
┌─────────────────────────────────────────────┐
│  J. M. Brown                    Postage       │
│  4 James Ave.                   Stamp         │
│  Reedville, N. J.                             │
│                                               │
│           Mr. Walter Craig                    │
│           2 Summit Terrace                    │
│           Portland, Oregon 97208              │
│                                               │
│  Personal                                     │
└─────────────────────────────────────────────┘
```

You will note that the ZIP Code has been inserted. The postal authorities urge the inclusion of this information as an aid to speedier and more efficient delivery of the mails.

THE HEADING

The heading, which is one of the standard parts of a letter, is at the upper right-hand side, and includes your address and the date. It should not be jammed against the very top of the sheet. An upper margin of at least one inch and a right-hand margin of about three-quarters of an inch should be allowed. This means that you must start your address, if in handwriting, well toward the middle of the top of the page.

Inclusion of Both the Address and the Date.   Sometimes, in a letter to a friend, the address is omitted and only the date or the day is given, perhaps not even that. It is just as well, however, to include both the address and the date, even in a friendly letter. Your friend may have forgotten your address. It is entirely possible, too, that he may wish to refresh his memory, for one reason or another, as to the date when you last wrote. He may even wish to keep your letters and enjoy rereading them later, in which event the dates would aid him in identifying the incidents you mentioned. (Of course, only the date is necessary if your address is engraved or printed on the stationery.)

The Month and the Year.   The name of the month should be spelled in full: *October, February,* etc.; and the year also should be written in full: *1963,* not *'63.* An abbreviation is all right in memoranda but not in correspondence. Except in very formal letters, do not use the ordinal numbers or an abbreviation of them (*first, second, 1st, 2nd*). Write, for example, *December 1, November 3.* The addition of *st, nd, rd,* or *th* after *1, 2, 3, 4,* and so on, is no longer considered desirable.

The Address.   As mentioned earlier, names of cities, even if long, should be spelled in full, but names of states may be abbreviated. Since it is not easy to remember the correct

abbreviations for our many states, territories, and possessions, the principal approved shortened forms are listed
below for quick reference. Note that Idaho, Iowa, Maine
and Ohio are omitted, since it is customary to spell these
names in full, even though sometimes *Idaho (Ida.), Iowa
(Ia.), Maine (Me.),* and even *Ohio (O.)* are abbreviated.

Ala.	Md.	Oreg. (or Ore.)
Ariz.	Mass.	Pa. (or Penn.)
Ark.	Mich.	P. R. (Puerto Rico)
C. Z. (Canal Zone)	Minn.	R. I.
Calif. (or Cal.)	Miss.	S. C.
Colo.	Mo.	S. Dak.
Conn.	Mont.	Tenn.
Del.	Nebr.	Tex.
D. C. (Dist. of Columbia)	Nev.	V. I. (Virgin Islands)
Fla.	N. H.	Vt.
Ga.	N. J.	Va.
Ill.	N. Mex.	Wash.
Ind.	N. Y.	W. Va.
Kans.	N. C.	Wis.
Ky.	N. Dak.	Wyo.
La.	Okla.	

The names of other insular possessions, and of Alaska,
Hawaii, and foreign countries, are spelled in full. It is best
to spell in full the words *Road, Boulevard, Square, Building, Place, Avenue,* and *Street.*

The following is a correct form of heading, with block
style and open punctuation.

427 John Street
Belleville, N. Y.
March 4, 1963

THE INSIDE ADDRESS

The inside address consists of the name and address of the
person to whom you are writing. (Your own address, remember, is called the heading of the letter, discussed just above.)

The inside address is customary in business correspondence but is not generally used in a letter to a friend.

Its use is proper, however, in some letters requiring a touch of formality, as, for example, in a letter you might write to someone whom you had heard on the radio, and whom you wanted to compliment or perhaps to question; or in a letter of appreciation to a speaker or performer who had appeared at your church or club; or in a letter to a prominent person whose opinion on an issue or event you wish to obtain.

The inside address may be used, also, in a letter from one club official to another, or from a club secretary to a guest whom he is inviting to appear at a club meeting. Such letters are sometimes called official or semiofficial. A letter to a Senator or a Representative, or to the President of the United States, should carry an inside address. It may precede the greeting, or salutation (see the next topic), as in business letters, or it may be written in the lower left-hand corner, below the body of the letter.

> 2 Haddon Place
> Hillsdale, N. J.
> March 14, 1963

The President
The White House
Washington, D. C.

Sir:

Respectfully yours,

Note that the greeting or salutation ("Sir:") to the President is correct as given above. Another correct form is: "My dear Mr. President." In this letter, the block form with open punctuation is used, and the inside address is placed, as in business letters, immediately before the salutation. The following letter is another of the same general type. In this correspondence, to a Congressman, the indented form is used, with closed punctuation, and the inside address is placed below the letter proper:

2 Haddon Place,
Hillsdale, N. J.,
October 14, 1962

My dear Mr. Smith:

Very truly yours,

Hon. William W. Smith,
    House of Representatives,
    Washington, D. C.

Again, remember that the envelope address and the inside address should be the same, in both substance and form.

GREETING, OR SALUTATION

As the term implies, this is your opening greeting to the person to whom you are writing. You use it just as you would address a person, formally or informally, face to face, before you enter into conversation with him. Further, as in that case, so in correspondence, the degree of formality will differ according to how well you know the person. In correspondence you should maintain a degree of formality with all except those whom you know very well.

Dear and *My dear*.   One inconsistency of English usage is the fact that, although *My dear* would seem to be a more intimate form of address than *Dear,* just the opposite is the case. You address a friend, *Dear Jim,* but an acquaintance, *My dear Mr. Jones*. In informal correspondence, you should use, in the salutation, the same name that you use in talking with the person. If the letter is to a close friend and you know him by a nickname, you may use that: *Dear Chubby,* or *Dear Slim*. Again, *Dear Aunt Flo,* or *Dear Uncle Freddie* —the same names you would use in chatting with them. Those with whom your acquaintance is more or less formal you may address as: *My dear Mr. —, Dear Mr. —, My dear Mrs. —, Dear Mrs. —,* etc.

Capitalization. Every noun in the salutation should be capitalized, as well as the first and the last word, and, of course, all titles, such as *Mr., Mrs., Professor, Captain, Bishop, Dean,* etc.

Informal Letters. Even in informal correspondence, do not use greetings such as *Friend Paul, Dear Miss,* or *Friend John.* Such salutations give an impression of cheapness and poor taste. In writing to one who is very dear to you, naturally you may use any intimate form of greeting you wish, observing the rules of capitalization discussed just above: *Dearest One, My very own Darling,* or any other endearing title.

Position. The salutation should be about one-half inch below the position reserved for the inside address at the top of the page. In social correspondence the greeting ends with a comma.

BODY OF THE LETTER

This is the main content of the letter—the "meat." It constitutes the whole purpose or object of the correspondence. Remember this from beginning to end, all the time you are writing, and make your letter clear and direct. Let it express sincerity throughout, whatever its particular subject or purpose: to offer an invitation, to express sympathy, to congratulate someone on a special occasion, or just to "chat" with a friend and give him all the latest news.

The Use of "I." There used to be a hard-and-fast rule, "Never begin a letter or a paragraph with the pronoun *I*," just as there was a similarly hard-and-fast rule, "Never end a sentence with a preposition." As a matter of fact, these rules have been relaxed because they seemed too arbitrary and artificial. A letter in which you strictly avoid ever beginning a paragraph with the first-person pronoun is apt to become a rather stilted affair—especially if it is a letter to a friend or an acquaintance.

Nevertheless, it is not good taste to use the pronoun *I* a great deal in any letter, either social or business. In conversation, you do not enjoy listening to a person whose principal pronoun is *I*. Nor do you enjoy a letter in which the *I* outweighs everything else. Remember that, when you write your letters. Of course, in letters to friends of long standing you do not need to be too particular on this point, but even in such correspondence it is good taste to avoid undue repetition of the first-person singular pronoun.

Clarity. "Put yourself in the other person's place" is a common bit of excellent advice too seldom followed. It is particularly helpful in letter writing. If you heed this advice, you will make yourself entirely clear; you will say all that you mean to say, and, just as important, you will not say what you did not mean to say. You will not leave your reader to guess your meaning, or to try to "read between the lines." Moreover, you will express yourself in an interesting manner; you will not repeat yourself—a very boring habit with too many writers, as well as speakers. You will avoid hackneyed expressions, worn threadbare from excessive use, such as, "It's a small world, after all," "Two heads are better than one," "I don't know much about art, but I know what I like," "He's a chip off the old block," "Once bitten, twice shy." Such bromides are godsends for people who do not want to make the mental effort required to express an idea with some degree of originality.

If you put yourself in the other person's place, you will also make your letter "mechanically" and visually neat: if handwritten—clearly legible, not crowded, free of blots and of words substituted for words crossed out; if typewritten (sometimes even social notes may be typewritten) —neat in appearance, with a ribbon that makes the writing clearly visible, with no jumped capitals above the lines, and with no gaps from jumped spaces between the letters of a word or between words. Whether handwritten or typewritten, only the most informal letters may have insertions above the lines—words or phrases you originally omitted.

Value of Self-Criticism.   Some of the points just emphasized may seem trivial. They are not. It is surprising how
many letter writers make a bad impression because they
fail to give enough attention to some or all of these things.
One of the best safeguards is to give a special reading to
your letter before you seal it and send it beyond your
recall. It is at this time, especially, that you should put
yourself in the reader's place. Sit back, at leisure, and read
it as if someone else had written it and sent it to you.
What would *you* think of it? If honestly applied, that is
about as good a test as there is. Make use of it regularly
and sincerely, and you will find that self-criticism can be
truly valuable, in spite of many statements to the contrary.

The trouble with a great deal of self-criticism is that
there is too much self in it and not enough criticism. Make
it honest, and you will find that it will materially help
you to improve your correspondence. When you give your
letter a final critical reading, criticize it on all points: the
content; the expression; the "atmosphere"; the layout, or
mechanics. The following are questions you might ask
yourself about your letter.

Is it really interesting, or just dull and routine? Have I
talked about things that will interest the reader—not just
about my own affairs? Have I made correct use of the English language, and have I made myself *perfectly* clear—
not only so that I can be understood, but especially so that
I cannot be misunderstood? Is there an attractive "atmosphere" to my letter—a real personality behind it? Have I
observed the fundamental rules of mechanics that insure
a good-looking and technically correct letter? Have I written
legibly so that the reader will not be obliged to "translate,"
interpret, or just plain guess?

THE COMPLIMENTARY CLOSE

This is simply a graceful way of putting an end to your
letter. If you were talking with a friend or acquaintance,
you would end your conversation, not by just turning and

walking away, but with some kind of polite or friendly good-bye.

Punctuation. The complimentary close should end with a comma. Sometimes in very informal letters punctuation is omitted in both the salutation and the complimentary close, but this is not usual. At least two spaces should be left between the body of the letter and the complimentary close, which should begin about in the middle of the page. Capitalize only the first word.

Wording. The following examples indicate the kinds of wording used, which varies according to the formality of the letter and degree of acquaintance with the person to whom you are writing.

VERY FORMAL: *Respectfully yours, Yours respectfully, Faithfully yours, Very truly yours, Yours truly.*

LESS FORMAL: *Cordially, Cordially yours, Sincerely, Sincerely yours, Yours very sincerely, Always sincerely yours, As ever, Ever yours, Always yours.* You will note that, among these, there is a varying degree of informality. Naturally, you will make your choice according to how well you know the person to whom you are writing.

ENTIRELY INFORMAL: *With much love, Your loving son (daughter, nephew, etc.)*, *With all my love, Affectionately, Affectionately yours.* In family letters and other intimate personal letters, of course, any terms of affection and endearment are appropriate in the complimentary close. Naturally, the close for love letters can hardly be laid down in any set of rules or principles. The individual who is in love will doubtless have a lively enough imagination to devise appropriate terms of endearment.

THE SIGNATURE

Although at first one's signature might seem to be a matter of the utmost simplicity, requiring no discussion at all, such is not the case.

Position. First of all, the signature written in the wrong position makes a poor impression. It should be begun two

or three lines below the complimentary close, and a little
to the right so that it will end at or near the right-hand
margin of the letter. The signature should always be handwritten, in ink, and ordinarily no title is attached, though
in formal correspondence a doctor may add *M.D.* or a
minister *D.D.* (if he has the degree of Doctor of Divinity) :
William M. Mason, M.D., or *Henry T. Walsh, D.D.* The
full middle name is signed if the individual is accustomed to
using it—otherwise not. If there are only two names, be sure
to spell out the first name—just the initial is not in good
taste.

Women's Signatures.   Regarding a woman's signature,
there are several points to be carefully observed. Here again,
the degree of formality determines the exact form of the
signature.

A single woman will sign formal correspondence with her
formal signature. It may be two names: *Mary Hemingway;*
three names: *Mary Edna Hemingway;* or first name, middle
initial and last name: *Mary E. Hemingway.* In very informal letters, she will use her first name only. To close
friends she may be known as *May* and will use that form.

A married woman's formal signature will be her full
name (first, maiden, and married) : *Ethel Mount Brown.*
Her maiden name may be omitted in the case of rather
informal letters: *Ethel Brown.* In very informal letters,
her first name, or a nickname by which she is known to
close friends, will be used.

A divorced woman may legally reassume her maiden
name, in which case she naturally reassumes the signature
she used before her marriage. If she prefers to do so, however, after her divorce she may use the same signature she
used while she was married. Thus, Ethel Mount, divorced
from John Brown, could sign her name as *Ethel Mount
Brown.* Formal reference may be made to her as *Mrs. Mount
Brown.*

Legibility.   Finally, let us repeat that the signature should
always be *clearly* written. When you come right down to it,

you are doing your reader a discourtesy if you give him or her the task of "unscrambling" a signature that is practically illegible. After all, if you were asked what your name is, you would not mumble it behind your teeth so that it could not be heard by the person who inquired. Sign your name so that it is perfectly clear to anyone who can read. This applies whether the communication is social or business, formal or informal. Incidentally, it is often the practice, in business letters, to have one's name typed under the hand-written signature to make sure that the reader will recognize it. You will be wise if you write so that no such artificial aid is necessary.

TYPEWRITTEN LETTERS

Now a word or two about typewritten social correspond-ence. As we mentioned earlier, even social letters may some-times be typewritten. Strange and radical changes are taking place in the modern world, and this is one of them. Until recently, probably because of the complete association of the typewriter with business, its use in social correspond-ence was considered extremely bad taste. But now, its con-venience, its neatness, its legibility, its accuracy for arrang-ing a letter on the page—all these factors have combined largely to break down the former hard-and-fast prejudice against such use.

Advantages.   After all, the typewriter does not dim the personality of the writer or lessen interest in what he has to say. If used skilfully, it improves the appearance of a letter and does away with the necessity of stopping to decipher any difficult handwriting. There is also the advantage that with a typewriter you can easily make a copy for your files. Even with social letters, a copy may be helpful to refresh your memory of what you have written. The copies will show how often you have written to a friend.

Increasingly in the future, the typewriter will probably be used for social correspondence by people who can typewrite well. Others, even though their handwriting may not be above reproach, had better continue using pen and ink. Formal notes, however, should always be handwritten.

Form of Typewritten Letters. Single spacing is ordinarily preferable to double spacing. Begin the body of your letter just below the salutation. Each new paragraph should be indented five spaces; the body of the letter should be indented one inch, or more if the letter is a short one. Allow two spaces between paragraphs.

2

Form in Business Letters

AS IN the case of social letters, the initial effect produced by business letters is very important. The paper and envelope introduce you, so to speak, into the office of the person to whom you write. If your letter does not make a good impression, even before it is opened, it may fail of the reception you want it to have.

A businessman's secretary is expert in judging the mail, and a communication arriving in a cheap envelope, perhaps addressed in poor form, will prejudice her against it. If, when she opens it, the paper and the form bear out her first impression, your letter may be given a place in the day's mail where it will receive a "later reading." If such a letter goes directly to the businessman himself, the impression is apt to be even worse. Therefore, treat first things first; choose paper and envelope with care.

PAPER AND PAGING

Paper. The paper used should be a good white bond, and generally of standard business size (8½ by 11 inches) with an envelope to match. The better the quality, the more effective the impression.

Note that we said the paper is generally of standard business size. In this modern age, some firms adopt a letter paper similar to that used in social correspondence, perhaps square in shape. It is difficult to avoid the impression that such a procedure is somewhat of an affectation. We shall confine ourselves here to standard business practice.

The matter of having paper and envelope match and fit

18

is of more than a little importance. Business offices sometimes receive letters on paper which does not match the
envelope in kind and quality, and which has had to be
folded in a special way to fit. It is hardly necessary to emphasize that such "misfits" are bad taste and bad business.

Paging. The paging and sequence of the business letter
do not permit the variation allowable in the case of social
letters. If a letter exceeds one page in length, the next page
is simply another sheet, in regular sequence. In proportion
to the total number of business letters written, not a great
many are longer than one page, since single spacing, almost
universally practiced, makes it possible to include much
material on one page.

If, however, your communication runs more than one
page, you should number each succeeding page in the
upper right-hand corner, placing immediately before the
page number the name of the person to whom you are writing. There should be a margin of about $\frac{1}{4}$ inch at the right
of the page number. Placing of name and number at the
top of the page is advisable in order that any pages which
get scattered or misplaced may be immediately identified.

The letter should be neatly folded twice, to make three
laps, or folds, each lap of about equal width. Thus it will
fit neatly into the long envelope commonly used for business correspondence. It is a convenience to the person opening the letter if you make the second fold so that it comes
a fraction of an inch below the top of the page. This leaves
an overlapping edge which can be grasped for quick and
easy unfolding. To fit a large sheet into a small envelope,
fold the sheet in half (horizontally) and then fold it twice
from right to left.

THE ENVELOPE

As with social correspondence, so with business letter
writing, the completeness and clarity with which the envelope is addressed are important factors. They are even
more so in business than in social correspondence.

First of all, be sure that you always have your return address on the envelope. This should be on the front, in the upper left-hand corner. You will remember that in social correspondence it may be on the back of the envelope, but for business letters the front is better. The return address should be consistent in form with the inside address. Include the ZIP Code in your return address.

The name and address of the person to whom you write should be placed halfway between top and bottom of the envelope, or a little lower, and should be begun approximately in the center. Allow about half an inch between the address and the stamp. The postal zone, if any, or the R.F.D. number should be included to facilitate the quickest possible handling and delivery.

If the street has a number—not a name—which consists of not more than two figures, you may spell it in full. For example, *243 Fourth Street,* or *67 Thirteenth Street.* These forms look better and make easier reading than *243 4th Street,* or *67 13th Street.* Of course, when the street number contains three figures, it is desirable to write it in figures: *421 125th Street.* The address is ordinarily written in three or four lines: names; street address; city, state, then ZIP Code. If there is no street address, put the city and the state on separate lines.

Any special information may be placed in the lower left-hand corner of the envelope as, for example, the name of a certain individual if your letter is addressed to a company but is to be read by that individual, *Attention: Mr. Samuel Smythe;* or perhaps the floor on which the office is situated, *Twenty-second floor;* or the department in which your addressee works, *Production Department;* or, if the letter must be read only by the person addressed, *Personal* or *Confidential.*

Following, then, is an example of an envelope properly addressed. We shall assume the block form for both envelope and letter, and single spacing, which represent the usual business practice.

Walter D. Hays   Postage
421 Elm Street   Stamp
Arlington, N. J. 07010

                    Mr. J. S. Walters
                    Acme Brick Company
                    62 Main Street
                    Weiser, Idaho 83672

Advertising Department

THE HEADING

If you can afford the expense, which is considerable, en-graved stationery is the best for business letterheads, and for envelopes, too. It carries with it an impression of quiet elegance and dignity that may go far toward gaining favorable attention at the very beginning. Next best is neatly printed stationery. An expert printing job can closely resemble engraving, and a businessman is not going to examine your letterhead closely to find out which it is. If you cannot use either engraved or printed stationery, then at least be sure to typewrite your envelopes in correct form, neatly and accurately.

The Engraved or Printed Heading. Of course, if an engraved or printed letterhead is used, that gives all the information required in the heading except the date, which is typed in, generally at the right, an inch or so below the heading; sometimes in the center. As you no doubt have noticed in receiving business letters, there is an almost endless variety in the form and make-up of letterheads— in the placing of the different parts, the amount and nature of the material included, and the amount of artistic elaboration, including color.

Some firms and individuals make the serious mistake of cluttering up the letterhead with entirely too much detail —a condensed history of the firm, names of officers, location of branch offices, slogans, pictures of factories, and so forth. Such a procedure is by no means necessarily a true indication of the size and importance behind the display. In this connection, it is interesting to note that Montgomery Ward, one of the largest firms in the world, has used for its letterhead just two lines in the top center of the page—the first line, *Montgomery Ward;* the second line, *Chicago 7.*

In the present discussion, we shall not go into the matter of elaborate letterheads. Consultation with a first-rate business stationer is by all means advisable regarding such details. We give here the fundamentals, and go on the assumption that the letter is typed, and block-spaced, with open punctuation, the most common arrangement. We present here what is simple and correct, without implying that other forms more varied and elaborate are not also correct in some circumstances.

The Typed Heading. The simple and effective heading, then, should have the name of the firm or individual at the top center, from one to one and a half inches below the top of the page; one space below, street address; one space farther down, city, or town, and state with ZIP Code number, if any. Two spaces below, centered, you may place the telephone number. If you type the date in the center, place it two or three spaces lower.

Another arrangement might be to type the telephone number at the left, about two or three spaces below the heading, and the date exactly opposite, on the right. In this case, leave the same margin at the left of the telephone number, and at the right of the date—about three-quarters of an inch. This arrangement will make a pleasing and well-balanced appearance in relation to the heading.

The following examples illustrate what has been described above.

JOHN SIMMONDS BROWN
48 Grove Street
Middlebury, Vt. 05753

October 9, 1962

JOHN SIMMONDS BROWN
48 Grove Street
Middlebury, Vt. 05753

October 9, 1962

JOHN SIMMONDS BROWN
48 Grove Street
Middlebury, Vt. 05753

Orchard 4–6281   October 9, 1962

THE INSIDE ADDRESS

The inside address, in its most detailed form, may consist of as many as six lines; in its simplest form, as few as two. Whether simple or complex, it should be the same in content and in form as the address on the envelope, whereby the Post Office is enabled to deliver your letter to the right person at the right place.

The two-line address is sometimes sufficient when the letter is sent to a very small town where everybody is known, or to a prominent federal, state, or municipal official.

Mr. William Pettit
Tom's River, N. J.

or

Secretary of the Treasury
Washington, D. C.

Probably the most common is the three-line address.

Mr. Arthur B. Purdy
224 Maple Avenue
Portland, Maine 04101

The inside address should include the title of the individual if he is an important officer of the organization. This title should immediately follow the name of the individual, provided it is not so long that it would extend far across the page and look awkward. Here is an example of a four-line address.

Mr. Oscar H. Monroe, President
Acme Copper Works
309 Highland Avenue
Los Angeles, California 90058

The following illustrates a five-line address, with a long official title on a separate line.

Mr. Herbert L. Winthrop
Assistant to the Sales Manager
Century Clothing Company
123 32nd Street
Portland, Maine 04101

A six-line address could be arranged like the following example.

Mr. Edward T. Zabriskie
Director of Public Relations
Social Activities Group
The Church Federation
18 West End Avenue
Duluth, Minnesota 55801

We have mentioned the advisability of placing a man's title on the second line if it would unduly extend the first line. But occasionally some line other than the first will be so long that it would present a poor appearance "in one piece." In such a case, it is permissible to break the line and indent the second part several spaces.

Mr. Jay Brown
Department of Construction
    and Public Works
Town of Millville
Somerset County, Maine

Abbreviations. These are a matter of choice sometimes, but not always. You may or may not abbreviate the following: Ave. (Avenue), Blvd. (Boulevard), St. (Street), Sq. (Square), Bldg. (Building); Hon. (Honorable), Rev. (Reverend), Rt. Rev. (Right Reverend), Prof. (Professor), Sec. (Secretary), Vice-Pres. (Vice-President), Pres. (President), Mgr. (Manager); geographical location as part of an address, N. Minton Ave., E. Halsey Blvd.; and names of most of the states, territories, and possessions (see list given in Chapter I).

On the other hand, there are certain well-known abbreviations which are standard. A few examples are: Mr.; Mrs.; Sr.; Jr.; Esq.; C.O.D. (Collect on Delivery); F.O.B. (Freight on Board); A.V. (Authorized Version); M.D. (Doctor of Medicine); Ph.D. (Doctor of Philosophy); C.P.A. (Certified Public Accountant); A.M.A. (American Medical Association); A.F.L. (American Federation of Labor); C.I.O. (Congress of Industrial Organizations); F.B.I. (Federal Bureau of Investigation); and many other short forms for well-known titles and names.

Accuracy in Spelling Names. In the matter of company names, follow the exact official form used by the company. If, for instance, the word *Company, Corporation,* or *Incorporated* is officially abbreviated, then follow that form in your inside address, as well as on the envelope—otherwise, spell it in full. Be very careful to spell the company name correctly. Few errors make a worse impression than a misspelled name.

This is perhaps even more important in the case of an individual. Everyone is "touchy" on this score. No one likes to have his name mistreated in any way—typographical errors; misspelling; or the use of any form other than the one the person himself customarily employs. A man may sign his name in some way that strikes you as extremely informal for a business letter, so you decide to be properly formal. In replying to Joe Travers' letter, you perhaps use the name *Joseph* and create an impression that may harm your business relations. Let his signature be your guide, and you cannot go wrong.

Attention Line.   Now a word about what is sometimes called the *attention line*. It may be used to call special attention (*a*) to the particular subject of the letter, or (*b*) to a company officer or employee whose special attention you want your letter to receive. In the latter case, the idea is that you are writing not to the company alone nor to the individual alone, but to the company, with special emphasis on the fact that you wish the individual to give your letter a special reading.

To call attention to the special subject of the letter, it used to be customary to preface the subject with *Re:* (Latin for *concerning*), and to place it on a line with the salutation, a few spaces to the right.

Model Paper Company
18 Market Street
Tipston, Oregon

Gentlemen: *Re: Sampson Contract*

The *Re:* is old-fashioned and should be omitted.

If the purpose is to obtain the special attention of an individual, the form below should be used.

Model Paper Company
18 Market Street
Tipston, Oregon

Gentlemen: *Attention: Mr. John Brown*

Another method, preferred by some authorities, is to place the attention line between the inside address and the salutation, even with the left-hand margin, with two spaces above and below it. This arrangement has the advantage that reference to a special contract, order, or the like can be placed on the salutation line, if so desired.

Model Paper Company
18 Market Street
Tipston, Oregon

Attention: Mr. John Brown

Gentlemen: *Sampson Contract*

Note carefully that, if the attention line is used, the salutation is to the company, not to the individual named in the line—that is, *Gentlemen,* not *Dear Mr. Brown.* A mistake is frequently made in this respect.

We have discussed the attention line at some length because it is often used, and it should be correctly used. There is some justifiable doubt, however, as to its necessity. After all, a letter can be written to the company and, at the beginning, a special request can be made that Mr. Brown give it his personal attention. As to devoting a special attention line to the subject of the letter, that seems hardly necessary if the correspondence is directly to the point and well written. The nature and importance of the subject can and should be made clear very early.

Position of Inside Address.   The exact placement of the inside address is particularly important because, once made, it determines both the up-and-down spacing and the left-hand margin of the letter proper. Since you want the finished product to give a pleasing, well-balanced appearance, the inside address should be considerably lower if the letter is to be brief than if it is to be long. Otherwise the letter will end too far up on the page.

There is no hard-and-fast rule as to where to start the inside address—in a long letter, not less than two spaces below the level of the date line; in a short one, considerably farther down than that, in order that not too much white space may remain below the end of the letter. The left-hand margin, like the vertical placement, of the inside address may vary according to the length of the letter. Even in a long one, the left-hand margin should not be less than one inch; it may be slightly more. In a very brief letter, the left-hand margin may be considerably more than one inch if necessary for the appearance of the whole set-up on the page.

The regular position for the inside address is just above the salutation, but, as in social correspondence, it may occasionally be placed after the close of the letter, at the left margin, two spaces below the level of the signature. This is not customary in ordinary business letters—only in those that are of an official nature, as, for instance, a letter to an officer of a club or to a government official, or perhaps in a letter which, while it deals with business, partakes of a personal flavor.

THE SALUTATION

The term "salutation" means just that—a greeting at the beginning of your communication. The idea behind it is to avoid the abruptness which would otherwise mark the absence of such a preliminary step. If you began without the salutation, a good many people would feel offended.

Special Points.   First, it is well to avoid the utterly rigid and impersonal *Sir, My dear Sir,* or *Dear Sir,* except in cases of extreme formality. Even if you have never met the man to whom you are writing, he will be pleased to be addressed by name, rather than by just a "tag." The use of his name creates a friendly atmosphere at the start.

Secondly, at the other extreme, there is at least a trend toward the omission of the salutation. The trend is not yet substantial enough or far enough advanced to establish usage, but it is worth noting and watching. However, a radical departure from habit and custom is slow to take root, and a good many people feel that to start right in with the message of your letter under the inside address is going a little too far. It is also true that those who omit the salutation often begin their letter in a "breezy" sort of way, to compensate for omission of the salutation, and the breeziness is apt to be overdone. Many individuals dislike, even resent, that kind of approach in a business letter, sometimes received from a writer whom they may have never even met.

Position of Salutation.   Probably the best position of the salutation is two spaces below the inside address, with the body of the letter beginning another two spaces below. This arrangement gives an appearance of compactness—an impression that inside address, salutation, and body are all integral parts, as they are. Further, there is not a crowded look, as there is when only one space separates (a) inside address and salutation and (b) salutation and body. Sometimes more than two spaces are left between inside address and salutation, but only two spaces between salutation and body. This arrangement does not seem advisable, for it leaves the inside address too isolated. In any event, the salutation, like the inside address, should begin exactly at the left margin, and a colon should follow it.

When the letter is such as to permit placing the inside address at the end of the letter (left margin), then the salutation can be typed, still at the left margin, a number of spaces lower than the date-line level. The exact number of spaces cannot be specified. You must determine that in relation to the length of the individual letter.

Singular or Plural.   The majority of business letters are probably addressed to an individual, and of course in such cases the salutation is singular. If, however, they are addressed to an organization, such as a committee, a board of directors, a club, etc., then the salutation is plural.

In this connection, if you are about to write to some group, it may be worth while to find out the name of an officer of the organization and address him personally. Your letter is likely to receive better attention and to produce more effective results than if addressed merely to the group In the latter case, too, there is always the possibility that it may not be passed on to the proper person.

Variety of Salutations.   There is some variety possible in the choice of salutations for business letters written to an

individual. Here are some of the possibilities. The order of
the following four groups, as well as the order within the
groups, represents a sequence from informal to formal:
(1) *Dear John: My dear John:* (2) *Dear Smith: My dear
Smith:* (3) *Dear Mr. Jones: My dear Mr. Jones:* (4) *Dear
Sir: My dear Sir: Sir:* Salutations to women are based on
the same principle, only the terminology differing. Note the
following examples: (1) *Dear Helen: My dear Helen:*
(2) *Dear Mrs.* (or *Miss*) *Smith:* (3) *My dear Mrs.* (or
Miss) *Smith:* (4) *Dear Madam: My dear Madam: Madam:*

The plural salutations are few, and are less frequently
called for than the singular. When writing to a group or
organization—corporation, company, board, committee, etc.
—composed of men, use the salutation, *Gentlemen,* or *Dear
Sirs.* This is proper even if the management includes some
women. If your letter is written to an organization composed
entirely of women, the proper form is *Ladies,* or *Mesdames.*
The latter is perhaps a little strained, but it is correct. If
you do not know whether or not the official group includes
women, you should use *Gentlemen,* or *Dear Sirs.*

Capitals and Abbreviations.   In the salutation, of course,
always capitalize the first word and the names of individuals.
You should also capitalize the words *Sir* and *Madam* and
any titles used in connection with a person's name. As the
first word, *Dear* is capitalized, but note carefully the fact
that it is *not* capitalized unless it *is* the first word. Note, for
example, *Dear Sir,* but *My dear Sir.* Although this may seem
like a small point, it is a very important one. Any instance
of wrong form in the brief salutation, on a line by itself,
stands out like the proverbial sore thumb.

Abbreviations are not in order in the salutation. This does
not mean that *Mr.* and *Mrs.* should not be abbreviated.
They always are, wherever they appear. One other title,
Doctor (*Dr.*), may be abbreviated, but even that may also
be spelled in full. In fact, used as it is in the salutation, with
nothing but the person's last name, it is perhaps better
spelled out.

THE BODY

As already stated, single spacing is generally used in business letters. Although for very short letters double spacing is sometimes employed, it is not common. If, however, double spacing is used for a brief letter, paragraphs must be indented. Never use the block arrangement (flush with the margin) with double spacing. In the following discussion, we shall assume single spacing.

The body of the letter may begin one space below the salutation, and there need be only one space between paragraphs. With single spacing, there is a choice between block and semiblock styles of set-up. Both are used a great deal, probably the block more than the other. Both give the same general appearance. In block arrangement there is no indenting of paragraphs, each beginning at the left margin as previously established. In the semiblock set-up, the beginning of every paragraph is marked by an indention, varying from five to ten or even more spaces.

Planning for General Appearance. A reminder is in order at this point. While certain definite suggestions and practices are given throughout regarding indentions and placement of the entire letter (heading, date, inside address, etc.) on the page, they are not to be taken as hard-and-fast rules. It is the principles rather than the rules that count— the principles of balance on the page, neatness, and pleasing appearance. Various adjustments of the factors mentioned may have to be made, according to the length of the letter. For example, a comparatively short one with heading, date, inside address, and salutation all close to the top of the page, and an indention of only one inch for the block paragraphs, may leave so much white space at the bottom as to give a bare, unpleasing effect.

In other words, those factors must be considered, *before* the letter is typed, in relation to how the letter will look *after* it has been typed. A high degree of proficiency will come with practice. The right-hand margin is established by the position of the date, which is typed so as to end flush with that margin, and by the length and desired placing of your letter on the page.

The Two-Page Letter.   In this connection, a letter may be long enough to require more than one page (sometimes only a little more). First of all, for the second page use a sheet of plain paper, not a letterhead. About one inch from the top of this second page, type the name of the person or firm that is the addressee, and the figure 2 (for the page number). These may be placed at the extreme right of the page, thus:

Mr. John Brown—2

but it is better still, as an identification if the letter gets misplaced, to include the date also on the second page.

Mr. John Brown   —2—   October 4, 1962

When the letter runs only a little more than one page, it is best, for the sake of appearance, that there be at least three lines on the second page. This will mean that the first page must be arranged accordingly. The heading, date, inside address, and salutation may be set lower, and the left-hand margin may be made wider, than for a one-page letter, in order to throw at least three lines of material over to the second page.

Variations in Form.   There is a variation of the block letter, not as yet used a great deal, in which the complimentary close and the signature are also aligned with the left margin, like the rest of the letter, except the date. The visual effect of this set-up is too much "left-handed" for the most pleasing appearance. A still more radical variation of the block form is an arrangement in which, in every paragraph, each line except the first is indented several spaces. Neither of these departures is in common use, and neither is particularly recommended, since they do not offer any real improvement.

Paragraphing.   Proper paragraphing of the letter is important from two standpoints: appearance and reader convenience. A letter composed of only two or three lengthy paragraphs does not look as neat and attractive as one broken into three or four. Moreover, comparatively short paragraphs are more easily read and more quickly understood than long ones. Especially the first and the last paragraphs should be relatively brief.

The Carbon Copy.   Be sure to make a carbon copy of every letter. Even the best memory may at times fail, and it may become necessary, long after you have written, for you to *know* exactly what you wrote. Unfortunately, there are people who may misquote and take advantage of you unless you can prove exactly what you did write. Again, someday you may want to pursue further an idea mentioned in some letter that you have written to the same person, and in such an event a carbon of your previous correspondence may be helpful.

THE COMPLIMENTARY CLOSE

Earlier, we compared the salutation of a letter to the greeting you give a person before you talk business with him. It is a touch of courtesy which prevents an impression of curtness or abruptness. Similarly, the complimentary close is comparable to a few polite words of farewell at the conclusion of a business conference.

Placement.   As in the case of all the other parts of the letter, the complimentary close should contribute to the general effect of pleasing balance. To that end, it is usually placed two spaces below the final line of the letter proper, and begun about in the center of the page. A close like *Very respectfully yours* takes much more space than *Sincerely* and therefore might be begun a little to the left of center, while *Sincerely* may well be started a little to the right of center.

For the best appearance, the complimentary close should

not end far on the right-hand side of the page; it should never extend beyond the right-hand margin of the body. If a letter is very short, sometimes the complimentary close may be placed more than two spaces below the letter proper. If this is done, however, be sure that all the rest of the letter is spaced and arranged in such a way that the close will not appear to be isolated.

Types of Complimentary Close. If you are very well acquainted with the person to whom you write on business matters, you may use a close that is quite informal. We shall concern ourselves here, however, only with the more frequent situation in which at least some degree of formality is in order. While, among the various types of close, there is not a great variety, there is enough to make possible considerable choice according to how formal you want to make your business letter.

A special point to be remembered is that, whatever complimentary close you use, it should be in keeping with the kind of salutation with which you open your letter. For example, if you use the formal and impersonal *Dear Sir* as the opening, you should close with a similarly formal, *Truly yours,* or *Very truly yours,* not with a friendly, informal *Very cordially yours.*

It may be said that the close which omits *Yours* is less formal than the one which includes it; and that, when *Yours* is included, it implies less formality when used at the beginning of the phrase than when used at the end. As basic words in the complimentary close, *cordially, sincerely, truly,* and *respectfully,* in the order here set down, indicate a gradation from the informal to the formal. When *very* is used with an informal close, it becomes still more informal; and *very* used with a formal close makes it still more formal.

Among the following you will find the most commonly accepted forms of complimentary close for business letters. Study them in relation to the principles explained above. Which of them would be best for very formal letters?

Cordially	Yours respectfully	Yours very sincerely
Sincerely	Sincerely yours	Very truly yours
Yours truly	Cordially yours	Yours very respectfully
Respectfully	Yours very truly	Very cordially yours
Yours cordially	Respectfully yours	Very sincerely yours
Yours sincerely	Yours very cordially	Very respectfully yours
Truly yours		

Some Special Points. Now a few special reminders regarding the complimentary close and certain matters related to it.

The participial ending, hanging in the air, is no longer considered good usage: "Hoping that I may hear from you soon, I remain . . ."; or, "Trusting that this will meet with your approval, I am . . . " If you have something like that to say, make a sentence of it, and then follow it with the complimentary close proper.

I hope that I may hear from you soon.
                                        Very sincerely yours,

Avoid the use of the obsolete "and oblige." It belongs among such "museum pieces" as "Your obedient servant." Instead of:

Kindly give this matter your prompt attention, and oblige
                                        Yours very truly,

just insert a period after "attention" and omit the words "and oblige." It is perfectly obvious that prompt attention will oblige the person requesting it.

In the complimentary close, do not capitalize any word except the first. "Yours very respectfully" is correct—*not* "Yours Very Respectfully," nor "Yours very Respectfully"; "Yours respectfully"—*not* "Yours Respectfully."

Never use the word *respectively* for *respectfully*. Perhaps in your case the warning is entirely unnecessary, but the mistake is so frequently made, and so serious, when it is made, that it should be mentioned here.

Never use an abbreviation in the complimentary close. You cannot afford to do so, for any such absurdity as *Truly yrs.* or *Yrs. respectfully* gives an impression not merely of carelessness but even of illiteracy.

Always end the complimentary close with a comma. This rule applies universally, no matter which kind of punctuation (open or closed) is used in the inside address.

THE SIGNATURE

It is really astounding to note the weird and fantastic symbols that often appear as signatures on business letters. They can no more be deciphered or "translated" than the signs on a totem pole. All the worse, such signatures sometimes appear with no typed duplicate under them, and without the writer's name on the letterhead. In brief, the reader may have no idea what the name is.

To put the matter bluntly, it is an act of discourtesy for anyone to write his name as illegibly as that. If you cannot read a person's signature, how can you address him in answering his letter? In your own letters, even if your signature has been typewritten under your writing, sign your name clearly, and also evenly—not on a slant. (In typewritten letters it has become a commonly accepted practice to typewrite the writer's name under his handwritten signature.)

Signature and Responsibility. In business correspondence the signature does more than merely indicate who wrote the letter. It indicates, too, who stands primarily responsible for what is written—the individual representing the company, or the company as such. If the company name is typed first, just above the personal signature, that means the company is primarily responsible for the content, and the individual only incidentally so. If, on the other hand, the letter, on a company letterhead, is signed by an individual, with his official standing typed below, perhaps with the firm name also typed underneath that, then the responsibility for the contents is his.

In the first case, below, the company, to all effects and purposes, signs the letter. The italics indicate a handwritten signature.

> (1) Very truly yours,
>   John Brown, Inc.
>
>   *William White*
>
>   William White
>   Treasurer

In the second case, herewith, the writer of the letter is the responsible party in the correspondence.

> (2) Very truly yours,
>
>   *William White*
>
>   William White, Treasurer
>   John Brown, Inc.

We are assuming the single-spaced block letter. Hence the signature, with the typed elements, is arranged in block form, like the inside address. In case (1) above, leave two spaces between the complimentary close and the company name. For the handwritten signature, three or four spaces should be left, in either case (1) or case (2), to avoid crowding. Sometimes even more space is called for, if the signature is large. Then, for the last two lines, use single spacing. Occasionally more than the two lines of data will be typed beneath the signature. In any event, use single spacing. It is common practice, relative to the signature, to type the initials of the signer at the left-hand margin, and about two spaces below the level of the last part of the typed signature, and to follow these with a colon and the initials of the typist. One space below, at the margin, may be typed *Enclosure,* if the letter includes one. Usually periods are not placed after any of the initials, and the typist's initials are generally not capitalized. Thus, if William White wrote a letter with an enclosure, and it was typed by Ethel Mayer, the lower left-hand margin will look as follows.

WW:em
Enclosure

If circumstances prevent the writer from reading or signing the letter, the person who takes the responsibility for him should sign the writer's name and then typewrite his own initials right under the signature. It is not necessary to use *per* before the initials.

Very sincerely yours,

William White
S.S.

William White, Treasurer
John Brown, Inc.

To facilitate a proper reply to her letter, a woman should identify herself as such and indicate whether she is married or single. She should not sign her surname preceded only by initials—*J. B. Doe* for *Jane B. Doe*. The typed part beneath the handwritten signature should indicate, in parentheses, the marital status.

Unmarried or divorcée with maiden name legally readopted	*Jane B. Doe* (Miss) Jane B. Doe
Married	*Mary Belle Dix* (Mrs. John A. Dix)
Widow	*Florence C. Downs* (Mrs. Arthur A. Downs) or *Florence C. Downs* (Mrs.) Florence C. Downs

Divorcée	*Alice Jones*
	(Mrs.) Alice Jones
	or
	Alice Jones Ayre
	(Mrs.) Alice Ayre
	but not
	Alice Ayre
	(Mrs. Robert D. Ayre)

No part of the signature—neither the handwritten nor the typed part—should run beyond the right-hand margin. In block letters, you may align your signature with the complimentary close at the left; in indented letters, you may indent your signature a little if this does not carry it beyond the right-hand margin. If your handwritten signature is very short, it is also permissible to center it under the complimentary close, and if it is very long, it may be started at the left of the complimentary close so that it will end at or near the right-hand margin.

A person's title or position should never be placed on the same line as the handwritten signature.

Except for articles, conjunctions, and prepositions, all words stating the title, position, or rank of the signer should be capitalized. "The" is capitalized if it is an official part of the company name.

It is an outmoded custom to type the word *Signed* immediately before the handwritten signature.

THE LETTER IN GENERAL

The following points relating to the entire letter should be carefully observed. Negligence with respect to these matters often mars what would otherwise have been a job well done.

Accuracy. You should strive for accuracy not only in mechanical and technical details but especially in references and statements, dates, spelling (especially names of persons and of firms), the use of language and punctuation, and arguments. In all things be accurate. It is much better to rewrite a letter than to send it out containing dubious or incorrect material.

Thoroughness. When you read your letter over before releasing it—and you always should—make certain that you have covered all essential points. If you are writing a reply to a correspondent, be sure that your answer is comprehensive and covers any questions that he expressed or implied. Don't make it necessary for him to write again for information you ought to have given him.

Conciseness. Some people who believe in being concise have the mistaken idea that they must be curtly abrupt. This is far from the case. In a business letter, each sentence must be grammatically complete, and each paragraph must deal adequately with its main point. But a concise sentence, paragraph, or letter need not lack completeness or courtesy. It merely omits wordiness, repetition, and nonessential "trimmings" in the form of a long-drawn-out beginning or ending. In being concise you will make friends, not lose them.

Clarity. To write a letter that will be clear to the receiver, you *must* first have a definite idea of what you mean to say. If you are vague in your thought, how can you expect the reader to grasp it immediately, as he should? To be clear does not necessarily mean the use of a great many words to express an idea. It means using the right words. Read your letter over before sending it, and don't be satisfied unless and until it possesses clarity.

Promptness. If you cannot answer a letter promptly, acknowledge its receipt and state that you will give it your early attention. Include a courteous expression of thanks for the letter.

THE POSTSCRIPT

A postscript may serve a useful and legitimate purpose in briefly re-emphasizing something in the letter, or in calling attention to something that has a connection perhaps indirect but still important. Some maintain that a postscript should never be used, but this attitude seems unduly arbitrary.

If used, it should be brief. It may start at the left margin, two spaces above the identification initials, and the message should begin immediately after the *P. S.* If the message runs for more than one line, the overrun should be indented where the message proper began.

P. S. You will note that our new West Coast office is strategically situated in relation to transportation.

Sometimes the *P. S.* with its message is placed where the identification initials generally come, in which case the latter are typed two spaces below the *P. S.*

3

Punctuation, Usage, and Spelling

EVERY LETTER should display at least an elementary knowledge of punctuation, correct usage, and spelling. Errors in these matters may make it difficult for the reader to grasp your meaning and often may distract his attention from your message. If you keep striving for correctness in all your writing, you will soon use the correct forms habitually. It will then be easy for you to follow the proper standards.

PUNCTUATION

Since correct punctuation is essential to good letter writing, either social or business, and is called for even on the envelope, we shall briefly review the minimum requirements. You may well refer to this section often and to advantage, and, when you come to the examples of good letters (in Parts Two and Three of this book), you may compare them with the principles explained here. In that way you will not only become familiar with good punctuation but will also fix in your mind the reasons for each form—that is the best possible way to remember the forms.

Much has been written about hard-and-fast rules of punctuation which are to be learned by "brute force," and which often are not too clear to begin with. In this book, on the contrary, we wish to emphasize the simple idea that one should concentrate on the *meaning* and forget about rules. Good punctuation carries with it certain additional

42

meanings that are not conveyed in the word symbols themselves. It often serves the same purpose as voice inflection in speech. For example, note the difference of meaning in the following, according to the punctuation: "He won." "He won?" "He won!"

From the standpoint of meaning, therefore—one definite meaning for each punctuation mark—good punctuation is easy to master. Thoroughly understand the meaning of each mark, fix it firmly in mind, and then use punctuation to write exactly what you mean. In the following pages, you will find an explanation of what each mark means and an illustration of its correct usage.

Beginning and End Punctuation. This is used to show the reader where one sentence ends and another begins. Without it, sentences would run together in a hopeless jumble. Four familiar marks are used to separate sentences.

THE PERIOD. This means, "A complete sentence ends here." Do not confuse it with the *abbreviation point,* which is used for an incomplete word symbol (Dec., for December), or with the *decimal point,* which is used with certain figures (4.001).

THE EXCLAMATION POINT. This mark means that the idea immediately preceding is to be given great emphasis. In speaking, you might provide similar emphasis by adding a remark such as "Believe it or not!" The exclamation point has the same effect in writing. Do not make too free use of this mark. The exclamation point should be reserved for really important occasions.

THE QUESTION MARK. As the name implies, the question mark indicates the end of a sentence which asks a question: *Why did he do it?* Note that a whole question may sometimes be implied, and very effectively, in one word: *Honestly?* (*Do you honestly mean that?*)

THE BEGINNING CAPITAL LETTER. This symbol means, "A new sentence starts here." It marks the start of a new sentence just as the period marks the end. *They entered the valley. Here was the climax of their journey.*

SENTENCE FRAGMENTS.   There are certain *sentence frag-ments,* or incomplete statements, which make sense by themselves, and which are very commonly used (a word, phrase, dependent clause). In any such case, treat the fragment like a complete sentence, and use appropriate beginning and end punctuation. Thus: *Not a chance. Help! Why that?* Do not overdo sentence fragments. In each case, make sure your meaning is clear.

The Five Principal Interior Marks.   Besides the begin-ning and end punctuation, explained above, there are five principal *interior punctuation* marks.

Inside the sentence, especially if it is long, sometimes the words alone cannot make the meaning perfectly clear. Thus, for clarification, we use various punctuation marks. There are five basic ones most commonly used in ordinary writing. Master these thoroughly and you will know the fundamentals of good punctuation. Note that three of the five basic marks consist of the comma symbol, either alone or in combination. Each, however, is a separate mark with a distinct meaning of its own.

THE SINGLE COMMA.   This means, "Here a small element has been omitted." It is used comparatively seldom, and the reader can always supply the omitted element easily for himself: *To advance was difficult; to retreat, (was) impossible. He was large, well-built, handsome.* In the sec-ond example, each comma represents an "and" omitted. In such a series sometimes an "and" is used before the last word of the series, for smoother reading, but even then it is better to insert the extra single comma: *He was large, well-built, and handsome.* Some editors omit the final comma. Note especially, however, that when any element in the series is a compound, the final comma is necessary. Thus: *He had red, pink and yellow, green, and gold bal-loons.* If the final comma here were omitted, you would have "green and gold balloons," which might mean a com-bination color. In brief, it seems best always to use the final comma.

THE PAIR OF COMMAS. Perhaps the most important punctuational symbol, this is the most frequently used of all marks of interior punctuation. It means, "The element set off by this pair of commas is not essential to the grammatical sentence structure, and, as placed, changes the normal order."

An English sentence has the following *normal order:* subject, with essential modifiers; verb, with essential modifiers; and object or verb complement, with essential modifiers. Now, you must use commas to "flag," or warn, the reader when you depart from the normal order by inserting a nonessential element. This is particularly important to remember because, owing to the structure of the English language, there are many and various instances of nonessential elements which break into and interrupt the normal syntax, or construction, and which therefore require the pair of commas. The following are typical examples of the principal cases.

1. Nonrestrictive clauses require the pair of commas. Such clauses interrupt the normal order.

> *Examples:* (a) The Secretary, who was also Treasurer, was always present at the meeting of the Board. (The dependent clause, separated by commas, does modify the subject but is not an essential modifier. The sentence would be perfectly clear if it were omitted. It breaks the normal order by separating subject from verb. Hence the pair of commas.) (b) He considered Jim, who had never failed him, the best friend he had.

Note, however, that restrictive clauses, essential to the meaning, are not set off by commas.

> *Examples:* (a) The friend who is not loyal is no friend at all. (The dependent clause in this case, too, stands between subject and verb but, since it is an essential modifier of the subject, there is no violation of the normal order. Hence, the pair of commas is not used.) (b) He shook hands with the man who was to be his partner.

2. Words in apposition are always nonessential, interruptive elements, and therefore call for the pair of commas.

Examples: (*a*) Mrs. James Hollingsworth, the hostess, made a speech of welcome. (*b*) Colonel William Arlen, officer in command, outlined the campaign.

3. Transitional phrases and words are merely connecting links between one idea and another. With no grammatical function, and no normal sentence position, they always separate two elements that belong together.

Examples: (*a*) This man, in brief, is guilty. (*b*) The plan, to be sure, seems worthy of consideration.

4. Words, names, or titles used in direct address are nonessential and always interrupt the normal order.

Examples: (*a*) This, my friend, is what I propose. (*b*) Wait, Mary, until I have explained. (*c*) Here, Captain, is the prisoner.

5. Conventionally regarded as grammatically nonessential elements interrupting the normal order are: the figure for a year immediately following a date within that year; and the name of a geographical area immediately following the name of a part of that area.

Examples: (*a*) He was born on October 12, 1884, at two in the afternoon. (*b*) His address is 218 Grove Street, Waltham, Massachusetts.

6. A direct quotation within a sentence is also regarded as a nonessential, interruptive element, although this usage seems purely arbitrary and conventional. A pair of commas is used.

Examples: (*a*) Nathan Hale uttered his immortal words, "I only regret that I have but one life to lose for my country," as the hangman's noose settled about his neck. (*b*) He was shouting, "I am innocent," as they led him from the courtroom.

It should be carefully noted that when the nonessential, interruptive element comes at either the beginning or the end of the sentence, only one part of a pair of commas is used. The other comma is absorbed, or replaced, by the beginning or the end punctuation.

> *Examples:* (*a*) To be sure, the evidence is all against him. (*b*) He is no superman, for all that.

Such nonessential elements (word, phrase, clause) change the normal order because, as emphasized earlier, normally the first thing in the sentence is the subject with its essential modifiers, and the last thing is the object or verb complement with its essential modifiers. Note the following sentences.

> *Examples:* (*a*) When he had locked the safe, he left his office for the night. (*b*) He left his office for the night when he had locked the safe. (No commas are used in the second example, because the modifying clause is in its normal position, exactly where it belongs.)

THE COMMA PLUS CO-ORDINATING CONJUNCTION. This is a mark normally used in only one situation, namely, in the middle of a compound sentence. It means, "One independent clause has now been completely stated, and another is about to begin."

> *Examples:* (*a*) He has done his best, but he has failed. (*b*) They cannot expect victory, for they have done little to achieve it.

THE SEMICOLON. This is a mark that has practically the same meaning as the comma plus co-ordinating conjunction. Either may be used to indicate the midpoint of a compound sentence.

> *Examples:* (*a*) He has done his best; he has failed. (*b*) They cannot expect victory; they have done little to achieve it.

In the use of the *semicolon,* however, there are two important variations:

1. If a sentence is complicated, a semicolon plus conjunction may sometimes be used instead of a comma plus conjunction, for the purpose of clarification, especially if the

sentence includes a considerable number of commas and therefore might be confusing if a semicolon were not used.

Example: The twilight was alive with a weird collection of bird, animal, and insect life, including great bats, swift and terrible, that swooped down on us without warning; and, as darkness fell, we were treated, if that is the word, to a symphony from an insect orchestra which, to say the least, was slightly out of tune.

2. If the elements in a series are long and complicated, one may sometimes use a semicolon instead of a comma (which indicates the omission of a conjunction between elements in a series).

Example: He had a record of two years in the Orient, filled with travel, study, and many thrilling adventures; three years in Europe, where, quite unexpectedly, he became involved in plots against royalty; and, as a climax, one year in African jungles, where, for two months, he was a captive of the natives.

THE COLON. This is equivalent to "in other words," "namely," "that is." It means, "What follows will explain more fully what has just been said."

Examples: (*a*) Here was his problem: he could make himself known and fight against odds, or keep quiet and fail in his mission. (*b*) The room contained just four articles: a chair, an old rug, a broken picture on the floor, and an ancient umbrella. (*c*) His achievement was remarkable: he had risen to great heights, in spite of handicaps that others had considered insurmountable.

It is customary to use a colon after the salutation at the beginning of a formal speech or letter, and after the word, Resolved, introducing a resolution, as in the case of the subject for a debate. All this is a matter of formal convention, rather than of punctuation. Note also its use after the word "Example," as employed in this discussion.

Examples: (*a*) Dear Sir: (*b*) Mr. Chairman, Ladies and Gentlemen: (*c*) Resolved: That the commission form of government is the best for this town.

Other Marks of Punctuation.   These marks possess considerable importance, even though they are less frequently used.

THE SINGLE DASH.   This mark means exactly the reverse of the colon, namely: "This is a summary or condensation of the details just given." In other words, the detailed statement precedes the dash.

> *Examples:* (*a*) He could make himself known and fight against odds, or keep quiet and fail in his mission—here was his problem. (*b*) A chair, an old rug, a broken picture on the floor, and an old umbrella in one corner—just these four articles the room contained. (*c*) He had risen to great heights in spite of handicaps that others had considered insurmountable—his achievement was remarkable.

PARENTHESES.   When used to enclose any element in a sentence, parentheses mean: "The normal order of the sentence is here changed by the insertion of a nonessential element so phrased that it bears little or no grammatical relationship to the rest of the sentence." Parentheses are much stronger marks than the pair of commas. They mark a more abrupt break in the sentence with respect to the relationship between the elements.

> *Example:* The whole school (1200 pupils, that year) was struck by the epidemic.

PAIR OF DASHES.   This punctuation mark indicates an emphatic break. It says, as it were, "Here occurs a violent interruption, either emotional or syntactical, that disrupts the normal order."

> *Example:* The swift violence of the flood—the waters had risen six feet in as many hours—drove the inhabitants rushing from the town.

It should be carefully noted that sometimes only one-half of the pair of dashes is used. Such is the case when a sentence is violently broken off, never to be completed.

> *Example:* "Help! Help!" shouted the man on the ledge. "I can't—" The roar of the collapsing building drowned the rest.

QUOTATION MARKS.   As the term implies, these credit some person or other source with the material enclosed by the marks. They mean, "The enclosed element consists of the exact words of some person or other source that the author is quoting." Single quotation marks are used for a quotation within a quotation. If, as rarely happens, there is still another quotation, within the second one, double marks are again used. Other principal uses of quotation marks are: to enclose titles of magazine articles, slang used in formal writing, and ordinary words or expressions used in a special sense.

> *Examples:* (*a*) "I shall quote," said the prosecutor, "the very words he used: 'I'll see you dead, first.' " (*b*) "Our neighbor," said my grandfather, "used to say, 'My son always was quoting the Shakespearean line, "To thine own self be true." ' " Note that the sentence ends with three sets of quotation marks. (*c*) His article, "The Importance of National Defense," appeared in a leading magazine. (*d*) He was said to have acted the part of the "jerk" on the bell rope in a well-known play. (*e*) There could hardly be a "gentlemen's agreement" between those two.

BRACKETS.   These are used to enclose, within a quotation, an explanatory remark made, not by the speaker himself, but by the person who is quoting him.

> *Example:* The speaker went on, "The massacre of every man in Custer's command [some claim that one survived] was one of the great tragedies of the West."

If you should ever feel that parentheses within parentheses are called for, use brackets instead of the inner pair of parentheses, to prevent confusion.

THREE DOTS.   These indicate the omission of material from a quotation, generally because the part omitted is not considered essential to the particular context. They mean, "Here a certain part is omitted purposely, but without any suggestion of an abrupt or violent break." Contrast this with the dash, explained above.

Examples: (*a*) "I seem to be very tired, and I . . ." His voice faded away and he was asleep. (*b*) "Love the Lord, thy God . . . and thy neighbor as thyself."

Some Nonpunctuational Devices. Among these are the hyphen, the apostrophe, the abbreviation point, and the decimal point.

THE HYPHEN. Two or more words are joined into a compound word by means of this spelling symbol; it is also used at the end of a line when a word is broken into syllables.

Examples: (*a*) a two-by-four plank. (*b*) He had a wonderful surprise awaiting him. (*c*) thirty-three.

THE APOSTROPHE. This is another spelling symbol. It is used in contractions, possessives, and some plurals.

Examples: (*a*) don't; (*b*) the General's authority; (*c*) the soldiers' uniforms; (*d*) three A's.

Remember also the following nonpunctuational marks, which, in contrast to punctuation marks, were mentioned earlier: the abbreviation point (Y.M.C.A.) ; the decimal point (1.423) ; the comma-like symbol used to separate the parts of large numbers (123,481) ; and the capital letter used in proper names and at the beginning of a line of verse, thus:

> "The plowman homeward plods his weary wa
> And leaves the world to darkness and to me.'
> —Gr&

COMMON FAULTS IN USAGE

Just as in everyday conversation one is often surprised, and sometimes shocked, by errors in the use of the English language, so in both social and business letters many instances of bad usage occur. The following list includes some of the most objectionable common errors. In each *example,* below, proper usage is represented by the word (or words) in italics, and the use of the alternative word (or words) would be incorrect.

Adopt (adapt). *Adopt* means to make one's own, to accept. *Adapt* means to make to conform with, to adjust to.

Example: I shall *adapt* my methods to conditions.

Affect (effect). *Affect* is a verb which means to exert influence upon. *Effect,* the verb, means to make something a reality, to bring about.

Example: The mediators *effected* a settlement.

All ready (already). *All ready* means entirely prepared, or, as the popular phrase goes, "all set." *Already* means before now, by this time.

Example: He had *already* left.

All right (alright). Sometimes the one-word spelling of "all right" is used, but it is not strictly correct.

Example: That plan is *all right*.

At about (about). *At* refers to an exact place or time. *About* means approximate. *At* and *about* should never be used together.

Examples: He arrived *about* five o'clock. He left *at* six o'clock.

But what, but that (that). Generally this error is made in connection with the word *doubt*.

Example: There is little doubt *that* he will succeed.

Can't hardly (can hardly). *Can't hardly* involves a double negative and is therefore incorrect.

Example: I *can hardly* do it without help.

Continue on (continue). The *on* is unnecessary, for *continue* means to go on.

Example: I think the storm will *continue* into the afternoon.

Different than (different from).   Although *different than* is perhaps the more often used of these two expressions, it is none the less bad usage.

Example: Your standards are *different from* his.

Don't (doesn't).   *Don't* is a contraction of *do not* (plural) ; *doesn't* is a contraction of *does not* (singular) .

Example: It *doesn't* seem right.

Due to (because of).   *Due to* means owing to, or attributable to, something. It is used as an adjective, never as an adverb. *Because of* is used as an adverb.

Examples: His failure was *due to* illness. He failed *because of* illness.

Equally as (equally).   The *as* is superfluous.

Example: The two men are *equally* skillful.

Every one . . . are (every one . . . is).   The words *every one* are a singular construction and take a singular verb. Do not let intervening plurals deceive you.

Example: Every one of the two hundred animals *is* well fed.

First began (began).   The word *first* makes the sense repetitious and should not be used.

Example: He *began* his political career when barely out of college.

Free gratis (free *or* gratis).   Since *gratis* is the Latin word for *free,* the two words should not be used together. Either *free* or *gratis,* alone, is correct.

Example: He received his tuition *free.*

Generally always (generally *or* always).   These two words are often used together when *always* alone is meant. Together, they make no sense.

Example: He *generally* arrives on time.

Greatly minimize (minimize). *Minimize* means to reduce to the very least. Since you cannot do more than that, *greatly* is incorrect.

> Example: You *minimize* his ability. (Never write, "You greatly minimize.")

Infer (imply). *Infer* means to draw a conclusion from someone else's action or statement. *Imply,* quite to the contrary, means to give someone else a basis on which to found a conclusion.

> Example: By his own statement, he *implied* a guilty knowledge.

Know as (know that, *or* know whether). The *as* makes no sense and is entirely out of place here.

> Example: I don't know *that* (or know *whether*) this is the time to act.

Less (fewer). *Less* must not be used when the reference is to number. It is correct only when reference is made to amount or quantity.

> Example: This year we had *fewer* mosquitoes than last.

Liable (likely, apt). A very common error is made in the use of these words. *Liable* implies undesirable consequences. *Likely* simply refers to the strong possibility of an occurrence.

> Example: It is *likely* to be clear today.

Like (as). This is a very crude, but common error. It is surprising how many radio script writers, newscasters, and others who should know better, make this glaring mistake.

> Example: *As* I said, I will stand by you.

Me (my). Before a verbal noun, or gerund, the objective case is incorrect. The possessive is required.

Example: Will the Government approve of *my* going on this trip? (Other correct forms, instead of *my*, would be *your*, *his, our,* and *their*.)

Morning at a.m. (morning, a.m.). To use both in referring to time is to repeat oneself, since *a.m.* means "in the morning."

Examples: The office opens at 9 *a.m.* The office opens at nine in the *morning*. (*Not* at 9 *a.m.* in the morning.)

Nothing else but (nothing but). The "else" is unnecessary.

Example: *Nothing but* perfection is his ideal.

People (persons). *People* is correctly used only in a collective reference to a comparatively large group.

Example: Two or three *persons* saw the accident.

Providing (provided). *Providing* is not allowable for expressing a conditional arrangement or situation.

Example: I will go, *provided* I can bring my friend.

Reason is (*or* was) because (reason is, *or* was, that). *Because* should not be used, since *reason* in itself implies *because*. It calls for a "that" clause explaining what the reason is or was.

Example: He was defeated in the election. The *reason is that* he presented his case poorly.

Shall (will) and will (shall). Misuse of these words, which is responsible for some of the most common errors in usage, should be strictly avoided. *Shall* is used in the first person, singular and plural, to express futurity or expectation; *will*, in the second and third persons. Just the reverse is true when command or determination is to be expressed. In questions, it is correct to use the form that is logically to be expected in the answer.

Examples: I *shall* be leaving early. I think you *will* have trouble with your campaign. You *shall* do as I say. We *shall* depend on you. We *will* defend our principles to the last. *Shall* you be staying here long? (The answer expected is, "I shall" or "shall not.")

Stop (stay). *Stop* refers to cessation of previous motion or procedure, and should be only so used.

Example: He expects to *stay* here a week.

These (this) kind. There is really little excuse for making this very common mistake—using a *plural* modifier with a *singular* noun.

Example: *This kind is* made in the United States.

Try and (try to). *Try and* clearly implies that one accomplishes what he tries. *Try to* means something quite different. One may *try to* do something, but not succeed.

Example: I'll *try to* be there.

Uninterested (disinterested). *Uninterested* means having, or showing, no interest in. *Disinterested* means impartial, unprejudiced.

Example: A good judge is *disinterested* in the cases that he tries.

Wait (await). These words are not synonymous. *Wait* means simply "to stay," "to remain." *Await* means "to wait for," and generally there is an implication of something important about to happen.

Example: He decided to *await* further developments.

Want to (ought to, should). *Want to* is a peculiar usage which, if analyzed literally, makes very little sense. It is a colloquialism that should be strictly avoided.

Example: You *should* be very careful.

HACKNEYED PHRASES

We all know individuals who seem to have no originality of expression. They use one stale phrase after another. Hardly any of us, however, can "cast the first stone," for we, ourselves, may be guilty in a greater or lesser degree. For that reason we are presenting here some of the most overworked expressions. With these as a warning, no doubt you will recognize and avoid many others also.

You will note that not all the expressions given in our list are always to be avoided. But, by and large, the list represents usage worn out through old age and hard service. We have set them down at random, believing that it will be of interest to you to take them in no special order and, as you come to each, check your own tendency to use it.

I note from your letter	Kindly advise me
Please rest assured	Along this line
With your kind permission	For your information
I note that	At hand
Your letter received	Acknowledge with thanks
Yours received	Awaiting your reply
I take pleasure	Even date
Permit me to say	Thanking you in advance
I regret to state	Up to this writing
May I suggest	Re, or in re
I note with pleasure	In the not too distant future
In reply, I would say	Pleasure of a reply
Has come to hand	In due time
Hoping to hear from you	Kindly inform
Herewith please find	Enclosed herewith
Thank you kindly	At all times
I wish to inform	Answering yours
This will inform you	Drop me a line
Please do not hesitate	Take this opportunity
I have before me	I remain
In this connection	Await the pleasure of a reply
At the present writing	Your letter of recent date
I carefully noted	The party referred to
Thanking you for your courtesy	Please note
At the earliest possible moment	Let me point out
Enclosed please find	Referring to your favor
At an early date	Wherein you state
Trusting this will find you well	Said person stated
Contents noted	Have attended to same

SPELLINGS YOU SHOULD KNOW

Because good spelling plays an important part in effective letter writing, we are including here a list of words whose spelling sometimes causes trouble. Perhaps people who have little trouble with spelling judge too harshly those who do have difficulty. The fact remains that your letters, whether social or business, are judged in no small degree by how well or how badly you spell.

Some people just do not take the trouble to master certain words, believing the matter to be unimportant. That belief is far from the truth. Form, usage, expression—all these are vital factors in good letter writing, but you may excel in all these and still make a bad impression if your spelling is seriously deficient.

You will find the following list helpful if you make it a point to master any listed words that you ordinarily misspell. Concentrate on them, use them, spell them right, and you will improve your letter writing to no little extent.

abeyance	annihilate	capitol
absorbent	anonymous	ceiling
accede	antedate	census
accelerate	apologize	changeable
accessible	apparent	chauffeur
accidentally	appreciate	chrysanthemum
accommodate	arguing	clique
achievement	attention	collectible
acknowledgment	authorize	comparatively
acquiesce	baptize	complementary
adherence	benefited	complimentary
advantageous	bequeath	concede
advisable	bigoted	connoisseur
advise	bouquet	conscientious
advisory	breathe	consensus
aggravate	bulletin	contemptible
alias	bureau	convalescence
allege	calendar	convertible
allotment	capital	corps

council
counselor
courtesy
criticize
cynic
debutante
deceased
delivery
dependent
desert
despondent
dessert
destructible
development
digestible
disagreement
disappointment
discernible
discreet
disheveled
dispel
donor
economize
eighth
eligible
embarrassing
en route
envelope
equipped
exaggerate
excusable
exhilarating
exquisite
extol
facetious
facsimile
faux pas
fiery
foreboding
forehead

foresight
forfeiture
franchise
frivolous
fulfill, fulfil
gauge
genteel
gnarled
gorgeous
grammatical
grievous
guarantee
gullible
hazard
hoping
hygiene
hypocrisy
illegible
imminent
impede
inadmissible
incidentally
indispensable
inflammable
intercede
interchangeable
irresistible
itinerary
jeopardize
judiciary
juvenile
khaki
knowledge
laboratory
laryngitis
legible
libel
license
loose
lose

luscious
maintenance
mantelpiece
mileage
mischievous
misspell
morale
morocco
motley
murmur
naive
Negro
nickel
niece
nonchalant
noticeable
nuisance
nutritious
obsession
occasionally
occurrence
omitted
ordinance
parallel
perceive
permissible
plaintiff
precede
pretense
prevalent
principle
procedure
profited
prophecy
prophesy
pseudo
pungent
pursuing
questionnaire
quietus

quizzes
quotient
recede
recommend
relieve
reservoir
respectfully
restaurant
rhythm
riddance
seize
separate
shipped
siege
sincerely
sinus
sleuth
stationary
stationery

stucco
suing
supersede
suspense
sycophant
syllable
symmetrical
synchronize
synonymous
tendency
tonsil
traceable
transference
treatise
trousseau
tryst
tyro
ukulele

umbrella
unanimous
unique
unnecessary
upbraid
vaccine
vacuum
vanilla
vendor
vengeance
veterinary
vetoes
vice versa
vicissitude
villainous
weird
whereas
withal

Part Two

TYPES OF SOCIAL LETTERS

4

Invitations and Announcements

In the many kinds of social contacts that we all experience, invitations and announcements play an important part. Some are formal, more are informal, but in either case it is essential, for the desired impression, that the form be correct and the content gracious and pleasing. Even in the informal type, the degree of informality will depend on the nature of the occasion and the closeness of relationship between the writer and the recipient.

Since the cycle of correspondence includes the reply, we shall here present some typical replies to serve as a guide for that phase.

Most formal wedding invitations are engraved or printed. In such cases a good stationer should be consulted about proper forms. The following forms are approved. (Middle names are included for those who have them.)

WEDDING INVITATIONS AND REPLIES—FORMAL

Wedding Invitations—Formal

Mr. and Mrs. Alfred Kent
request the honor of your presence
at the marriage of their daughter
Jane
to
Mr. John Atwater
Monday, the third of May
at five o'clock
The Methodist Church
Hanson, Vermont

WITH RECEPTION CARD ENCLOSED.

Reception
immediately following the ceremony
32 Elm Street
Hanson, Vermont

R.S.V.P.

or

The favor of a reply
is requested

Or

Mr. and Mrs. Alfred Kent
request the pleasure of your company
at the wedding reception of their daughter
Jane
and
Mr. John Atwater
Monday, the third of May
at six o'clock
32 Elm Street
Hanson, Vermont

R.S.V.P.

Sometimes a separate card is also enclosed with these invitations.

At home
after the sixth of June
Jamestown, Rhode Island

FOR A HOME WEDDING.

Mr. and Mrs. Alfred Kent
request the honor of your presence
at the marriage of their daughter
Jane
to
Mr. John Atwater
on Monday, the third of May
at five o'clock
32 Elm Street
Hanson, Vermont

R.S.V.P.

Replies to Wedding Invitation—Formal

Mr. Frederick Morse
accepts with pleasure
Mr. and Mrs. Alfred Kent's
kind invitation to be present at the
wedding reception of their daughter
Jane
and
Mr. John Atwater
Monday, the third of May
at six o'clock
32 Elm Street
Hanson, Vermont

Mr. and Mrs. Ralph Mason
regret exceedingly that they
are unable to accept
Mr. and Mrs. Alfred Kent's
kind invitation to be present at the
wedding reception of their daughter
Jane
and
Mr. John Atwater
Monday, the third of May
at six o'clock
32 Elm Street
Hanson, Vermont

WEDDING INVITATIONS AND REPLIES--
INFORMAL

Wedding Invitations—Informal

TO A RELATIVE

Dear Aunt Flo,

On Tuesday, November the third, at four o'clock, Jack and I are taking the important step. We are being married at Saint Joseph's, that charming little church—you know it—at 14 Fenway Drive.

I hardly need to tell you that we would not consider it a

real wedding if you were not present. There will be an informal reception in the church parlor afterward, and we want you there, too.

> Always affectionately,
> Julie

To a Friend

Dear Bill,

Well, here's the good news for you, among the first. I suppose that you, as one of Harry's best friends, knew it was coming. Harry and I are getting married, and the date and place have been set. The wedding will be at Glenbrook Church, at three in the afternoon, December fourth, but it will be a quiet affair with only a few friends and relatives present. You, Bill, are one of the few.

We are counting on you, so please don't disappoint us. You must come to the informal reception, also, at my home. The occasion wouldn't be perfect without you. Be sure to say yes.

> Always your friend,
> Marie

To a Friend

Dear Bess,

Walter and I have decided on Thursday, April the fourth, as the date for our wedding. We both want an extremely simple ceremony, so we are going to have only our two closest friends present, and they will act as witnesses. The reception, at my home, at four o'clock, will also be of the simplest kind, with just a very few relatives and special friends invited. We certainly want you among that group.

Don't disappoint us. You know how much it will mean to us both to have you there.

> Most sincerely,
> Edith

Replies to a Wedding Invitation—Informal

Relative's Acceptance

Dearest Julie,

You have no idea what a thrill your note gave me. My Julie getting married, and to that wonderful man! You know how much I think of you both, and how many good wishes I am sending along right now.

Yes, indeed, I'll certainly be at your wedding, and at the reception, too. I wouldn't miss a minute of the occasion. And while there I'll hope to be brought up to date on all the family news. It's been so long since I've seen any of you. I had hoped to visit the family long ago, but one thing after another interfered with my plans.

Please give my love to your mother and father—and don't forget Jack. I'll be seeing you soon.

Lovingly,
Aunt Flo

FRIEND'S ACCEPTANCE

Dear Marie,

That certainly is good news, and for some time I had been hoping to hear it. Congratulations and all good wishes to you and Harry. I don't know any two individuals whom I'd rather see starting out together, and I don't know which of you is the luckier.

You may count on me—reception and all. It is good of you to say it will mean a lot to have me with you. For my part, it will mean a great deal to me to be there.

Again, heartiest congratulations to you both.

Cordially,
Bill

FRIEND'S REGRET

Dear Edith,

It is with the greatest disappointment that I have to tell you I shall be unable to attend your wedding reception on April fourth. You were so good to include me among your guests. Unfortunately, I have to represent my firm at a special conference in Chicago at that time, and I can't possibly change my plans to permit my return for the occasion.

My congratulations, and my very best wishes to you and Walter for all the years ahead.

Always your good friend,
Bess

BRIDAL LUNCHEONS AND SHOWERS— INVITATIONS AND REPLIES

Bridal Luncheon—Formal Invitation

Mrs. William Atterbury
requests your presence at a
Bridal Luncheon
in honor of her daughter
Janet
on Wednesday, January the second
at half after three o'clock
The Moon Room, Hotel Albert
Carrington, Maine

R.S.V.P.
24 Oak Drive
Carrington, Maine

Shower—Letter of Invitation

Dear Adele,

You remember that for some time I have been considering the idea of giving a shower for Jean. Well, I have now definitely decided to do so. The date is Monday, January the sixth. The time is three o'clock. The place is my home—you know where that is.

I plan to make it a kitchen shower, and I know that your experience as a married woman will inspire you to bring a gift that will be most welcome.

We shall try to keep it a secret until the big day. Be sure to come.

Cordially,
Winnie

Shower—Letter of Acceptance

Dear Winnie,

It will be a pleasure to be one of Jean's friends at the shower you are giving for her. Thank you for including me among the guests invited. And I think you are to be congratulated for your part in undertaking all the plans and preparations.

Incidentally, I have already thought of a gift which I am sure will please Jean and at the same time prove very useful.

I shall look forward to seeing you and all the others on the sixth.

Cordially,
Adele

Shower—Letter of Regret

Dear Winnie,

It is with real regret that I shall have to decline your very pleasant invitation to attend the shower for Jean on January the sixth. Some weeks ago, I agreed to visit my aunt on the West coast for the first two weeks in January. I have not seen her for a long while, and I fear I could not now change my plans.

To prove my good intentions, however, I am sending to you a small gift for Jean. I shall appreciate your giving it to her and, with it, all my good wishes for her future happiness.

Believe me, I shall be thinking of you all on that occasion.

Cordially,
Adele

INVITATIONS TO DINNER (FORMAL)
AND REPLIES

Invitation to Dinner—Formal

Mr. and Mrs. James Sturgeon
request the pleasure of
Mr. William Noble's company
at dinner
on Tuesday evening, August the first
at seven o'clock
1470 South Thomas Avenue
Bordentown

R.S.V.P.

Acceptance Note, Formal

Mr. William Noble accepts with pleasure the kind invitation of Mr. and Mrs. James Sturgeon to dinner on Tuesday evening, August the first.

Note of Regret, Formal

Mr. William Noble sincerely regrets that a previous engagement prevents him from accepting Mr. and Mrs. James Sturgeon's kind invitation to dinner on Tuesday evening, August the first.

Invitation to Dinner, Formal, To Meet a Special Guest

Mr. and Mrs. James Sturgeon
request the pleasure of
Mr. William Noble's company
at dinner
on Tuesday evening, August the first
at seven o'clock
to meet Mr. A. Eddington Carrol
1470 South Thomas Avenue
Bordentown

R.S.V.P.

Invitation to Dinner, Formal, On a Special Occasion

Mr. and Mrs. James Sturgeon
request the pleasure of your company
at dinner
on the Tenth Anniversary of their marriage
Saturday, the eighth of May
at eight o'clock
1470 South Thomas Avenue
Bordentown

The favor of a reply
is requested

Invitation to Dinner and Theater, Formal

Mr. and Mrs. James Sturgeon
request the pleasure of
Mr. William Noble's company
for dinner and the theater
on Monday, May the first
at seven o'clock
1470 South Thomas Avenue
Bordentown

Kindly respond

Cancellation of Dinner Invitation, Formal

Mr. and Mrs. James Sturgeon
announce with regret that
owing to sudden illness
they are obliged to recall
their invitation for dinner
on
Monday, May the first

MISCELLANEOUS FORMAL ANNOUNCEMENTS

Engagement Announcement—Formal

Mr. and Mrs. Arthur Kent
announce the engagement of their daughter
Miriam
to
Mr. Jonathan Board
on the fourth of October
one thousand nine hundred and fifty-one
in Evanston, Illinois

Wedding Announcement—Formal

Mr. and Mrs. Arthur Kent
have the honor to announce
the marriage of their daughter
Miriam
to
Mr. Jonathan Board
on the fifth of December
one thousand nine hundred and fifty-one
in Evanston, Illinois

Birth Announcement—Formal

Mr. and Mrs. Donald White
take pleasure in announcing
the birth of a son
John William
on Thursday, February the first
Nineteen Hundred Fifty-one

INVITATIONS TO DINNER (INFORMAL)
AND REPLIES

Note of Invitation to Dinner

My dear Miss Waite,

It will give Mr. Winters and me great pleasure if you and your fiancé, Mr. Trimble, will dine informally with us at our home on Tuesday, January the fourteenth, at seven-thirty, and spend the evening. If it is agreeable to you and Mr. Trimble, we plan to drive downtown after dinner and dance for a short time at the Hotel Singleton.

I hope that nothing will prevent your being with us.

Yours sincerely,
Dorothy Winters

Note of Acceptance

My dear Mrs. Winters,

How very kind of you to invite Mr. Trimble and me to dinner on the fourteenth of January. We are delighted to accept and, as we are both very fond of dancing, we know that the entire evening will be most delightful.

Sincerely yours,
Hilda Waite

Note of Invitation to Dinner and the Theater

My dear Mrs. Allerton,

Mr. Dennison and I should be delighted if you and Mr. Allerton will come to dinner Friday evening, October the twelfth, at six-thirty, and attend the theater with us afterward. I am writing some time ahead because, if you accept, I want to be sure to get tickets for the Theater Guild's presentation of *Hamlet*, which, as you know, is extremely popular.

We do hope that you will find it possible to be with us.

Cordially yours,
Clara Dennison

Note of Regret

My dear Mrs. Dennison,

Because of the necessity of your securing theater tickets well ahead of time, I feel I should let you know at once that

Mr. Allerton and I shall have to say "no," very regretfully, to your alluring invitation. We should have been happy to spend that pleasant evening with you and Mr. Dennison, but unfortunately there is uncertainty as to Mr. Allerton's business plans. He may have to be away at the time you mention, and I do not feel that it would be fair to you to delay a definite reply.

Thank you for thinking of us, and perhaps you will be kind enough to repeat your invitation at some later date.

Cordially,
Gertrude Allerton

Letter of Invitation to Dinner, to an Intimate Friend

Dear Amy,

You know how much both you and I have missed Belle Dutton since she married and moved to California. Good news! She and her husband are to be in town for a few days next week and they have accepted our dinner invitation for Monday, March third.

Bill and I want you and Jim to share the happy occasion. We hope that Belle's husband will tell us about his latest movie venture, and I know that we shall all have a wonderful time together. We just can't take "no" for an answer, so let us hear soon and please make it "yes."

Yours always,
Josephine

Letter of Acceptance from Friend

Dear Josephine,

Your irresistible invitation calls for just one possible answer —"yes." Of course, Jim and I will come and we can hardly wait for the day to arrive. I'll tell you a secret. We did have another engagement for the evening of March third, but we managed to change our date. So we'll be knocking at your door just before dinner.

It will be so good to see Belle again and to meet her husband. She will be kept busy bringing us up to the minute on all the news. Jim says to thank you, too. We'll be seeing you.

Ever yours,
Amy

LUNCHEON AND BRIDGE INVITATION
AND REPLIES

Letter of Invitation to Luncheon

Dear Kathy,

I hear that you are leaving in ten days for a month's vacation on the Cape. Certainly I envy you both the vacation and the place where you are to spend it. You know, that is familiar territory to me. I have been there a great deal, particularly at Chatham, where you are to stay. That is where I learned to swim and sail, and I count among my best friends many of the native Cape Codders, as well as a considerable proportion of the summer cottagers.

Won't you lunch with me Tuesday, June third, at Joe's Sea Food Restaurant—you know where it is—at one o'clock? We can enjoy just the right atmosphere there in which to talk over your plans, and I want to give you some introductions that will make your vacation the more enjoyable.

Cordially,
Doris

Letter of Acceptance

Dear Doris,

Your very friendly invitation is the perfect touch to make my vacation anticipations just right. And that idea of the Sea Food Restaurant for this particular occasion is so appropriate. It takes you to think of something like that. I remember the many happy luncheon meetings we used to have there—the quiet atmosphere and good food, the courteous waiters—just the ideal place.

Indeed I do accept with the greatest of pleasure. I'll be at Joe's, Tuesday, at one o'clock sharp. You are most kind to suggest giving me those introductions. I'm sure they will add a great deal to the pleasure of my stay on the Cape, for at present I have very few friends there.

Thank you for your thoughtfulness, and I'll be looking forward to seeing you.

Sincerely,
Kathy

Letter of Invitation to a Card Party

Dear Ella,

Bert and I had such a good time at your card party last month that we want to play host and hostess this time. Could you and Wayne come over Monday evening, December the second, about eight-thirty? We'll play either Bridge or Canasta, whichever you prefer. The Finnegans and the Nortons will be here, too. You know them, I believe, and they are all excellent card players.

The game and the evening would not be complete without you and Wayne. Please say you'll come.

Sincerely,
Sue

Letter of Regret

Dear Sue,

Wayne and I both appreciate your attractive invitation to play cards at your home on December second. We can't think of a pleasanter way to spend an evening, particularly as we are Canasta enthusiasts at the moment. Unfortunately, it will be impossible for us to be there with you. My Aunt Harriet in Illinois has asked us to visit her for a week, beginning December first. I haven't seen her for years, and we have already accepted her invitation. Bill is taking part of his vacation at this time, and he is really looking forward to a pleasant rest and change.

We both regret that we can't accept, and we do appreciate your thinking of us. Perhaps, after we return, you'll ask us again.

Cordially,
Ella

LETTERS OF INVITATION TO WEEK–END PARTIES, AND REPLIES

For a Yachting Week End

Dear Ed,

I know you're as fond of the water and the wide open spaces as I am, so I want you to share them with me over the week end of August third. You remember that I bought a thirty-five-foot yawl, with auxiliary motor, last spring.

I have her all tuned up and in fine condition, having already spent most of my week ends this summer cruising aboard her. She is a real yacht, with the best of seagoing qualities, and I know you'll enjoy taking your trick at the wheel. Like you, I don't like using the motor unless the wind fails.

John Bates and Fred Martin, old cruising mates, whom you know, will make up the foursome and you may be sure that we'll all have a good time. They are coming to the club with me from the office. If you can meet us at the 4:10 train for Bayside, Friday afternoon, we'll have dinner at the club and then go aboard. I plan to cruise to Huntington and back, if weather permits.

I certainly hope to see you "aboard the yacht."

Yours always,
Tom

Letter of Acceptance

Dear Tom,

It is indeed good of you to include me among your guests for the cruise over the week end of August third. You may be sure I'll be on hand and will meet you at the train as you suggest.

I remember with a great deal of pleasure the many good times we have had cruising together and, if I'm not mistaken, Bates and Martin were with us, two years ago, when we were nearly wrecked in that storm off Nantucket. It will be fine to have them along.

Thanks again, Tom, and I'll see you on the third.

As ever,
Ed

Letter of Regret

Dear Tom,

Thanks very much for the invitation to be your guest "aboard the yacht" over the week end of August third. You know, better than anyone else, how much I'd like to accept, but I'll have to say "no" this time.

Father is coming on from Chicago to be with me from the third until the seventh. I'm more than disappointed not to be with you, and I'd have been delighted to see Bates and Martin once more. I remember several occasions on which they were ideal cruising mates.

I wish you good breezes and fair weather. Please try me again before the summer slips away. Believe me, I'll do my best not to disappoint you next time.

Always yours,
Ed

Invitation to Prospective House Guest

Dear Cynthia,

First of all, welcome home! That is, welcome back to Belleville—next Sunday. I know that you'll be on a business trip as a professional buyer for your firm, and that you had to leave your family in Ohio. That's the penalty you pay for being an expert career woman.

There are many old friends just waiting for a chance to see you again. Glen and I insist on your making our home your headquarters for your four-day stay. It just wouldn't be right any other way! Then we can plan to invite some of your best friends to renew acquaintance. In that way, you won't have to take your brief time running here and there to see them. But don't worry—we'll not wear you out. We *will* leave you some time for your business.

Please make us happy by accepting this invitation. We are so sure you will that I am already getting ready for you the room you enjoyed so much when you used to visit us. I'm keeping my fingers crossed for the return mail, and I'm sure it will bring the good word.

As ever,
Maud

Letter of Acceptance

Dear Maud,

Your invitation, with the warmth of friendship that it contained, was one of the pleasantest things that ever came my way. I was hoping that I had not been forgotten in Belleville and now I am sure of it. Such a "welcome home" as yours indeed warms my heart.

Of course, I accept, and thank you very, very much. I can't tell you how much this means to me. Please thank Glen, too. It will be wonderful to see you both again and to have such an opportunity really to "catch up." You'll have to help me save enough time for my business, while I'm with you, or I may be a lady without a job when I return.

I'll look forward eagerly to seeing you next Sunday.

Yours affectionately,
Cynthia

5

Letters of Thanks

This type of letter should be, at least theoretically, easy to write. When someone has sent you a gift, done you a favor, shown you hospitality, or the like, it ought not to be difficult to express appreciation. The sample letters herewith may be helpful in indicating what else besides a mere "thank you" is properly included in this kind of correspondence. Such letters, if well written, are an excellent opportunity further to strengthen the friendship represented by the occasion for which you are expressing gratitude.

FOR WEEK–END AND OTHER VISITS

For Courtesy to Another

My dear Mrs. Weeden,

This letter is to tell you that your courtesy to my daughter last week, while she was in Los Angeles, was something that I shall never forget. I wanted her to call on you and remember me to you, but your insistence that she be your guest for four days really touched me. You certainly added greatly to the pleasure of her stay in the city.

The dance on Tuesday and the theater party on Thursday were experiences that Cora will remember for a long time. She cannot say enough about you and your friends. I know she has written you her thanks, but I wanted to add my own. I hope that I may have the opportunity some day to return your kindness.

Very sincerely yours,
Emma Hays

For Week End

Dear Sam,

That week end with you and Miriam was a treat long to be remembered. I have written her a "thank you," but I want to send you a special note for yourself.

It is so long since the days when we were in college together that my visit meant a great deal to me, permitting us, as it did, to catch up on the years between—and that isn't always easy. It was such a pleasure, also, to see how very happy you and Miriam are. Remember, I always told you that you'd find just the right girl, and you certainly did. I congratulate you again, Sam, and your wife, too.

Helping you with the building of that sun porch was great fun. You used to tell me I was good at that kind of thing. And that day's sail on the Sound was a rare treat. I'll dream about it on long, cold winter nights.

Thanks again, Sam, a million. Long life, prosperity, and happiness to you both.

As ever,
George

For Dinner

My dear Mrs. Winthrop,

It is a double pleasure to write my thanks for your charming hospitality at dinner last Wednesday. First, it is pleasant to express appreciation for such gracious entertainment. Secondly, in writing, I live over again an evening so delightful that I like to recall it as often as possible.

You were very kind to afford me the opportunity to meet James Waters. I had formed a flattering mental picture of that rising young author, and I must say that he more than made it a reality. You may be interested to know that he has sent me tickets for a lecture that he is giving next week. In fact, we had a brief talk about the topic of his lecture, and he plans to include some of the ideas which he and I discussed at the dinner.

Again, thank you most sincerely.

Cordially yours,
Fay Chalmers

FOR CHRISTMAS AND BIRTHDAY GIFTS

For Christmas Gifts

Dear Stan,

   You couldn't have given me anything that I wanted more or would enjoy more than that handsome desk clock for my office. And what a sly one you were! I remember your pointing out that very clock in the jeweler's window, a week ago, and telling me, "You ought to have one of those in your office, Claude. It would add to your prestige." Your beautiful gift will keep me right on time, from now on—and you must drop in soon and see the improvement in my prestige. I want to take you to lunch next week. Can you make it Monday, at one?

   Unless I hear to the contrary, I'll expect you then.

Yours,
Claude

Dear Uncle Tim,

   You always were my favorite uncle, and the reason is simple —there is no one on earth more thoughtful and generous. If Santa Claus ever were unable to make his rounds on Christmas Eve, I know he wouldn't even be missed if you would consent to step in and take over.

   Well, I just don't know how to thank you enough for that beautiful traveling bag, replacing the one I lost during my vacation last summer. It is an exact duplicate—something I thought I'd never have again. Believe me, I am not going to let this one out of my sight. It will be a constant reminder of you and, for that, I'll think all the more of it.

   Thank you very, very much.

With love,
Barbara

Dearest Claire,

   I won't say, "You shouldn't have done it," because that is a worn-out expression, but I will say that you were so generous that you took our breath away, accustomed as we are to your generosity. All members of the family are enjoying your gifts to the full—Rod, the two children, and I. We all thank you, and they are writing you separately.

My special thanks for the exquisite bracelet. It will remind me of you whenever I wear it, and I assure you I'll not often be without it.

I hope to see you at the Drama Club next week.

All my love,
Betty

Dear Aunt Polly,

You must be a mind reader, for that writing set that greeted me in the artistic package, Christmas morning, was the thing I wanted most of all. I am using it for the first time to write you my heartiest thanks. It seems as if you had a special talent for selecting the gifts people especially desire.

You will be glad to hear that I am to have a full month's vacation next summer, and I am planning to stop off and see you on my way to the West coast, where I shall spend most of my time.

With your present on my desk, I certainly have no excuse for not writing to you often, and to all my friends. You may expect to hear from me frequently.

Affectionately,
Bertha

For a Birthday Present

Dear Charlie,

I have reached the point where I had decided that I would not make very much of my birthdays, but you evidently do not agree with me. That beautiful wrist watch you sent me reminds me of my birthday, but it does more than that—it reminds me of how much a friend like you means, and always has meant, to me.

I can't tell you how much I appreciate your gift. It will always remind me of you—as if I ever needed anything to do that. Thanks, Charlie, more than I can say.

Yours as ever,
Bob

Dear Uncle Jerry,

Mother always tells me that I make more of my birthday than I do of Christmas. Maybe because you knew that, you

sent me such a very beautiful gift. Certainly it makes me feel
as if it were Christmas. Words can't express how I love the
ring, and how much I love you for giving it to me. It just
proves again what I've always said—that you are the best
uncle a girl could have.

I understand your next business trip will bring you within
a few miles of our town. You must plan to come and see us
then. This will give me a chance to thank you personally.

All my love,
Patricia

FOR WEDDING GIFTS

To Acquaintances

My dear Miss Wayland,

The wedding present you sent to Harry and me is one of
the most beautiful, as well as one of the most useful, gifts
we have received. That lovely flower vase, you may be sure,
is going to be much in evidence in our new home. It happens that Harry is one of the comparatively few men who are
enthusiastic about flowers—and you know what a flower lover
I am. You could not have given us a more welcome present.

You must come and see how ideally your gift fits into its
surroundings here.

Sincerely yours,
Esther Wellington

My dear Mr. Eddy,

It was most thoughtful and generous of you to send us the
handsome bridge table and chairs, which will play an important part in our married life. We like them especially because
they will be a very pleasant means of having many happy
gatherings with friends. Harry joins me in thanking you most
heartily for your thought of us.

We are both looking forward to having you as one of our
first guests at that table. You will hear from us again soon.

Yours gratefully,
Esther Wellington

My dear Mrs. Thompson,

Harry and I most sincerely appreciate the beautiful mono-
grammed crystal goblets from you and your husband. Wed-

ding presents are always exciting and yours gave us a thrill, I assure you. Among our gifts was a lace tablecloth with napkins, so you see how well the goblets will grace our dinner table. As you know, we both have many friends and shall be entertaining a great deal. You could not have given us anything that we could enjoy more.

When we return from our wedding trip, we hope to have you both dine with us, and we shall drink to your health from those lovely goblets.

Sincerely yours,
Esther Wellington

To Friends
Dear Don,

Your silver candlesticks are perfect, and I really mean just that. The design, the contour—everything about them makes them "a thing of beauty and a joy forever."

You know Harry admits his artistic sense is not all it might be, but you should have been on hand to hear his enthusiastic comments when I opened your box. He joins me in sending you our warmest thanks.

Cordially yours,
Esther

Dearest Louise,

Harry and I were overjoyed with the exquisite coffee service, which now holds a prominent place in our imposing display of wedding gifts. This beautiful remembrance of yours will be used and enjoyed constantly, with many pleasant thoughts of you.

We are only sorry that you no longer live nearby so that you could run in often and have coffee with us. Thank you again so very much, Louise.

Affectionately,
Esther

To Relatives
Dear Cousin Mabel,

How good you were to start us on our married life with that marvelous set of matched luggage! When Harry and I try to "take it all in," as we often do, it gives us ideas which I'm afraid are going to be hard to live up to. We see ourselves traveling abroad de luxe, for the best hotels are none too good for that luggage. Certainly it is going to make our honeymoon a very glamorous affair. I think we'll have to take many vacations, too, in order to keep it constantly in use.

Thanks seem very feeble for such a lovely gift, but we do thank you most sincerely. Your present will remind us of you for many years to come.

All my love,
Esther

Dear Aunt Rose and Uncle Tom,

My favorite aunt and uncle have certainly kept up their reputation for generosity and good taste in wedding gifts. Nothing could have pleased Harry and me more than your beautiful silver carving set. Believe it or not, it matches perfectly the set of flat silver from Harry's parents.

As you know, we love to entertain, and we shall be proud to exhibit your gift on many occasions. We hope that one of these will be the day you dine with us in our new home and see your gift in actual use.

Affectionately your niece,
Esther

Dear Uncle Ed,

Harry and I find an ordinary "thank you" entirely flat and inadequate as an acknowledgment of your wonderful wedding gift to us. The check you sent us literally took our breath away. If you only knew how much it means to us, you would be especially happy. As you know, we bought that house on Travis Street, and so we were going to be economical and not take a wedding trip. But now, thanks to you, we can, and we can also get some very special fittings and furnishings for our new home.

Your sort of kindness and generosity comes once in a lifetime, and we thank you from the bottom of our hearts. You are going to be our first guest at 28 Travis Street.

Affectionately,
Esther

6

Letters to Close Friends and Family

If any letters should be spontaneous, informal, and interesting, certainly they should be those to close friends and family. Yet, how often they sound "hard to write," stilted, and uninteresting. We cannot tell anyone just what to say in correspondence of this sort, which certainly should reflect the relationship that prompts it. Relax and write as you would talk, about things, events, and people of mutual interest.

The letters in this section are designed, not to tell you what to say, but rather to reflect an appropriate atmosphere and indicate effective language in correspondence with intimate friends and family.

LETTERS TO AND FROM ABSENT FRIENDS

To a Friend at a Distance

Dear Art,

I just can't get used to the fact that you're not in our old home town any more, nor in the office with me. Let's see, how long is it now since you left here? The calendar says it is eight months, and you can't argue with the calendar, though I'm inclined to do just that.

Neither of us is a very good correspondent, but I think it's my turn to write, and first of all I want to say, give me more news about yourself. Is the new job out there on the Coast proving worth your having made the move? Is the manager easy to get along with, and does he appreciate your talents and ability? I've heard he is rather "hard boiled." Have you found a good apartment? Last time you wrote, you were still looking. How about recreation? Is there a good bowling club for you to join? I know you'd be lost without one.

As for me, you'll be glad to hear that I am to be promoted next month—Assistant Sales Manager, no less! You'll have to address me as "Sir" after this. I'll get considerably more salary and that will be most welcome, with the cost of living apparently going up indefinitely. Don Mayer and I plan to spend our vacation together next summer at Lake Placid. He likes the outdoors as much as I do. Mabel Turner in our office— you remember her—has at last become engaged to Ted Macy, the Personnel Manager. We all saw that coming—or perhaps *he* didn't. And, oh yes, the town has condemned the property at 12 Walnut Street. About time, everybody says. It certainly was an eyesore.

Well, that's about all. How am I doing? Please do at least as well when you answer, and let that be soon, Art.

Always yours,
Ben

A Friend's Reply

Dear Ben,

You see, I'm answering you promptly this time, and let's both keep up a good schedule. I think, however, that letters mean more to me than to you, since I'm the one who has moved away. I really do appreciate your letters, Ben.

Now as to your questions. It is a little early to tell definitely whether or not the new job will be all that I hoped, but the future looks promising. Already, I have been able to save the Production Department a tidy sum by reorganizing methods and making certain shifts in personnel. The manager is appreciative, too. He is not as "hard boiled" as some make him out to be. Probably you, like me, have noticed that such is often the case. Regarding an apartment, the outlook is good. I've found one I want, and I think that I'll be signing up for it next week. I enjoyed all your news, especially the item about Miss Turner, with the accompanying comment.

By the way, let me know how young Jones is doing. They

took him on in the office, you remember, just before I left, and I was very much interested in him.

Write me again soon, Ben. In the meantime, my best regards to you. Please remember me to my other friends in the office.

Yours, as ever,
Art

Letter from Vacationist to Friend

Dear Ellen,

Well, here we are, Walt and I, at Edgartown, on Martha's Vineyard Island, and all our dreams of last winter are coming true.

The old houses and tree-shaded, narrow streets, with tar sidewalks that get soft on hot days; the bracing salt air, and the brilliant sunshine on sparkling water; the white sails offshore, and the little lighthouse standing sentinel at the end of a long breakwater; the town dock with the fishing boats that come and go—all these are only part of the fascination that is Edgartown. We only wish you could share it with us.

Then, too, there are attractive trips here and there. Gay Head, at the extreme tip of the Island, is one of the choicest spots of all. It is only about twenty miles from Edgartown, and well worth the trip. A lighthouse stands on the top of a cliff, widely famous for its varicolored sands, and the view is gorgeous—a great sweep of sea out to the arc of the horizon. I just can't describe the beauty of it. You have to see it and, when you do, you never forget it.

Walt and I are taking it easy, for the most part—not trying to follow any schedule or be too strenuous. We have rented a little Woods Hole catboat and enjoy sailing about the harbor and up into Katama Bay, where we go ashore, laze around on the smooth sandy beach, and revel in the magnificent ocean view. We swim every day from a beach near the harbor entrance.

Enough of us. Please write to give us all your news. I know you are leaving soon on your own vacation, and we are counting on your keeping us informed about all the good times you will certainly have in France and England.

Walt joins me in sending best regards and good wishes.

Affectionately,
Eileen

A Friend's Reply

Dear Eileen,

It certainly was pleasant to receive your breezy letter—and I do mean breezy. Right here in the hot city I could almost smell the salt air that you described so vividly. Evidently you and Walt have selected an ideal place for the kind of vacation you both like the best. I envy you, and it was all I could do to restrain myself from resigning and coming right up there.

Compared to all you told me, and the way you told it, my letter will be very dull, I fear. Just the old routine, with hectic days at the office, especially for me, as I am trying to put everything in perfect order before I leave. When I arrive home at night, often quite late, I am so weary that it is hard to work on my itinerary, which I must do if I am to make the most of this rare opportunity of a trip abroad. But everything will be worth while when I finally do leave.

You may be sure that I will write you en route, and I'll send you my various addresses as soon as I know exactly where you can reach me, and at what time.

Please remember me to Walt, and my best to you, as always.

Ever yours,
Ellen

FAMILY LETTERS

Letter from Father to Son at Camp

Dear Son,

Needless to say, your mother and I miss you at home, but we are happy that you are having such a fine, healthful summer at that beautiful lake, and with boys and counsellors who are the best kind of pals a fellow could have. We are delighted that Ben Simpson and Ted Sawyer, two of your old friends, are your tent mates.

The house is entirely too quiet without you—and I'll tell you a secret, just between you and me. Yesterday, when Mother and I were in your room, she said, "You know, this room is much too neat. I think I'll muss it up a little and make it seem as if Bill were home." So you see she misses you a lot, too.

Make the most of your summer, Son. It's a great chance to practice swimming. I think that, if you make real progress, I'll get you a sailboat of your own next summer, down on Barnegat Bay, and teach you to sail. But you must be a good swimmer first. Ten years old is none too young—so go to it.

Write soon again and give us all the camp news. Mother will write tomorrow. We both send you our love and constant thoughts.

Always devotedly,
Your Dad

Letter to an Absent Brother

Dear Chuck,

It is hard to realize that you have been in the West for three years now, and I'm glad we've kept up a fairly regular correspondence.

It is good to know that you have made such a success of your ranching venture. Pete Leonard was kind enough to drop in last week and tell me all about his visit with you. It was the next best thing to seeing you. He gave a glowing account of your accomplishments.

As I told you, some time ago, I decided to start a small advertising agency of my own. The reason I have not said more about it lately is that I wanted to be able to report real progress. Now I can. I have added three new accounts recently and the money is really coming in.

Last week I had the honor of being elected President of our local Kiwanis Club. That will mean considerable demand on my time, but I feel that my business will profit from the contacts I make in this way.

That's about all the news for now. Be sure to write soon and give me the latest about yourself. Pete asks to be remembered to you.

Yours as ever,
Larry

LOVE LETTERS

To a Fiancée

Sweetheart!

I wish I had a magic carpet so that I could fly the two hundred miles between us in a few minutes and then get back to my office before the manager noticed I'd been away. Honestly, Darling, this being so far from you is almost more than I can stand. I'm thankful that there are only two weeks more before we'll be spending that marvelous vacation together at your aunt's on the Maine coast. Then I can tell you how much I love you. A letter just can't express it.

Speaking of letters, bless you for writing so often. I know you are very busy with your work in the studio, as well as the planning for our wedding—in two months. Think of that! If you only knew how I'm counting the days and hours and minutes! Believe me, my dearest, it's true.

My next thrill is going to be the ring of the postman. I know that will mean another letter from you.

All my love, dearest Beloved.

Forever yours,
Gordon

Letter to a Fiancé

Gordon, dearest,

What a lovely letter! I agree with you about that magic carpet. It is just what we need right now to commute on and bring us together. I agree with you, too, Darling, about this long separation. It just doesn't seem right, when two people love each other as much as we do, that they cannot be together *all* the time.

But let's not think of that. Let's just think that in two short months we'll be saying "I do," and then *nothing* can keep us apart. And soon, that vacation—what a happy reunion that will be! We can then talk over all our plans for the honeymoon, and that will make the happy day seem very near, won't it, Sweetheart? As for writing so often—I couldn't stop if I tried, for then you *would* seem far away indeed, so you just keep watching for that postman.

Gordon, my Beloved, do get Elizabeth Barrett Browning's *Sonnets from the Portuguese* and read them. Just imagine that I am saying those words to you, for I mean them, every one.

All my love,
Edna

7

Congratulatory Letters

Letters of this type offer a real opportunity to draw friends and relatives closer together, to turn acquaintances into friends, to inject more of friendship into business relationships—in short, to practice that magic "human touch" that means more in life than most of us realize.

Such letters must, above all, be genuine and sincere. *Put yourself in the other fellow's place.* Enter into the pleasure, the pride, and the satisfaction that the particular occasion has given the person to whom you write. Remember also that, to be effective, your letter of congratulation must be written *promptly*—very soon after the particular occasion.

The letters that follow are meant to exemplify the principle that we have emphasized.

ON SPECIAL HONORS AND ACHIEVEMENTS

My dear Mr. Winthrop:

As a citizen of our town, and one who has its best interests very much at heart, I want to be among the first to congratulate you on your election as Mayor. The large majority given you by the voters proves that there are a great many like myself who definitely wanted our local government removed from incompetent, dishonest hands and entrusted to a man who is honest, efficient, and loyal to the highest standards.

You may count on me to help in any modest way I can.

Very sincerely yours,
John Bates

My dear Mr. Barry:

Only yesterday I saw in the business news that you have been made President of your firm, in whose success you have played such an important part. As one of your former employees, I offer my heartiest congratulations for an honor most highly deserved.

Please accept also my wishes for the very best in your future career.

Sincerely yours,
Alfred E. Morgan

Dear Professor Townsend,

It was a thrill and a pleasure to hear the radio announcement last night that you have been selected as one of the outstanding scientists of the year, for your work in physics. As one of your old students, I have sometimes thought that if you could teach me, you could achieve anything in your field. And sure enough, here comes this wonderful news!

Seriously, Professor, I can't tell you how delighted I am, and how proud to have had even a humble association with such a distinguished man. Please accept my heartiest congratulations. I know we shall be hearing much more about you.

Yours very sincerely,
Mary B. Ward

Dear Fred,

Well, I knew you'd get that well-deserved promotion! I just met Dave Winslow of your staff, and he told me that two days ago you were made Advertising Manager of the company. Fine work! Also, congratulations to the firm. I know that a more able man for the position could not have been selected.

You have my very best wishes for continued and increasing success.

As ever,
Dick

My dear Mr. Wainwright:

Permit me to congratulate you enthusiastically on your speech last night at Milton Hall on "Economic Problems of Today." I traveled a considerable distance to be present, and the effort was well worth while. We hear so many generalities of little value that your presentation was especially welcome and satisfying. I am glad to hear that the speech is to appear in *The Economic Review*.

You may recall that we met last month, in Washington, at the Willard Hotel. I hope we shall meet again soon.

Sincerely yours,
Robert A. Simms

ON A BIRTHDAY

To Friends and Relatives

Dear Joe,

Whether you like to remember your birthday or not, I do. In the case of a friend like you, I wouldn't think of letting the occasion go by without special notice. There are many others like me, too, who take a great deal of pleasure in telling you, at least once a year, what an unusually fine fellow you are. I know this hurts your modesty, but you'll just have to stand it.

In this same mail I'm sending you a little remembrance, which I hope you'll enjoy. Congratulations and best wishes, Joe, and may you have many more anniversaries.

Yours,
Howard

Dearest Fay,

It is always a pleasure to say "Many happy returns of the day" to a person like you. I sometimes think people don't even realize what the greeting means. Certainly when I say it to you it means, "May you be with us for many years to come!"

You know I don't often become sentimental, but on this occasion I want to assure you that our friendship is one of the prized possessions in my life, and that I treasure it accordingly. On your birthday I like to think back and enjoy again the many good times we have had together, and I'm looking forward to many more.

I hope you received the gift I sent. I thought it would go well with that blue dress you bought the last time we went shopping together.

All my love,
Peg

Dear Billy,

Here's a warm birthday greeting to a nephew who means a lot to me. I can hardly realize that you have reached your tenth milestone. Why, I can remember you when you were only—but boys of your age don't like to be talked to that way, do they?

It is with great pride that I have followed your record in school, as well as reports of you from home. Your devotion and loyalty to your wonderful parents are traits that unfortunately not all boys of your age possess. I am sure that as you grow up you will "go places," and I am going to enjoy your success with you, all along the way.

Congratulations, Billy, on "Number ten," and may you have many more. Watch for the postman. He's bringing you something that I think you'll like.

Lots of love,
Uncle Jeff

Dear Sis,

You see, your big brother doesn't forget the birthday of a very important person. I'm afraid I'm not a very good correspondent, but this occasion I certainly would not pass by. Many, many happy returns! I wish you would make known your secret of always staying young!

Do you still enjoy San Francisco? It is too bad that as a "career woman" you had to choose a spot so far from home. Here the old routine goes along pretty much the same as usual. Your old friend, Alan Forsythe, is getting married next month. The Andersons are moving to Wyoming—Mr. Anderson's business, the reason. And the Merriman's cat had kittens yesterday. I think I've covered the news. Now let's have some from you.

Use the enclosed check for something special—and think kindly of me.

Your devoted brother,
Hal

Dear Carl,

I'm sending this birthday note to reach you, I hope, on the important day. I hear they are giving you quite a celebration in the office, personal, as well as official, in honor of your recent promotion. Of course, I'll be there with bells on. But I wanted this to be a very personal greeting at your home.

Congratulations and all good wishes. It's the old friends like you who really count. I don't have to say much more than that —you know what I mean, Pal. You'll get my present at the office, along with the rest.

I'll see you soon. My best to Madge, and tell her from me she's a mighty lucky lady.

Always yours,
Doug

ON GRADUATION

Dear Carol,

As an old friend of yours who enjoyed the thrills of graduating from college some years ago, I want to be among the many who are congratulating you and wishing you the very best from now on. There is nothing else quite like college graduation and the big step out into the world of reality and hard facts, with the challenge that is always waiting there.

You have already shown such marked ability at Bryn Mawr that I know there are great things ahead for you. I'm glad you have chosen social work as your field. That certainly holds endless possibilities today.

Again, heartiest good wishes and please keep in touch with me. I know you will have interesting things to report.

Sincerely yours,
Clyde

Dear Gus,

Here's to you! My warmest congratulations on your graduation from Columbia. I'm glad we had two years there together, anyway. I have many pleasant recollections of our experience as roommates and of the fine times we had. Do you remember the night you were giving an imitation of our chemistry professor, in our room, and just then he walked in upon us? "Those were the days."

How does it feel to be a man of the world now? I know the world will be a little better for your stepping out into it, Gus. And I know, too, that in your chosen field of teaching you will make your mark. The profession needs many more like you.

As soon as you know, please tell me where you are going to teach. I want to keep in touch with you.

As ever, yours,
Jerry

Dear Babs,

I'm sending you, in this very special letter, very special love and congratulations on this very special occasion. You see, everything is very special. And why not? My only niece graduating from high school, and with honors! I think it's wonderful.

You have made a record to be proud of, and, with many others who think highly of you, I'm proud, too. I know you will keep up your fine achievements in the bigger world that's waiting for you. It is good news that you have been accepted at Wellesley. You couldn't have chosen a finer college, and its campus is one of the most beautiful anywhere.

Since you'll be traveling a good deal from now on, I'm sending you something to accompany you on your trips. Let me hear from you often.

Yours devotedly,
Uncle Eric

ON ANNOUNCEMENT OF ENGAGEMENT

Dearest Isabelle,

It was so good of you to write me that personal note, telling me of your engagement to Kenneth Smiley. Congratulations, my dear, to the lucky man, for he has drawn the prize of all prizes in you. I regret that, as yet, I do not know him better, but I certainly intend to, and hope that, in the future, we may become great friends.

All I need to know, dear, is that you've said "yes" to Kenneth. That, to me, is the best possible evidence that he's a wonderful man. I give you both my blessing and send you my warmest good wishes for a long life of happiness together.

Affectionately yours,
Anita

Dear Gerald,

Well, well, well! That's my first reaction to the great news you have just sent me of your engagement to Celeste Dupont. As an old pal of yours, I am very happy to know you'll have such a rare teammate in the double harness. There's nobody who deserves the best more than you—and now you certainly have it, believe me.

Please give my congratulations to Celeste also. I know she'll agree with me that they are in order. I am so glad I know your fiancée as well as I do. We both belong to the same drama group.

You both must have lunch with me some day at the Princeton Club. You see, I want to make it all official. I'll telephone you soon to set the day.

Always yours,
Hugh

Dearest Cecilia,

My little niece engaged! That is happy news, and I do appreciate your including me among the very first to hear of it. I have read your long letter three times, already. It is so much like *you* that I felt as if you were right here with me, bright and happy and bubbling over, telling me all about everything.

Billy must be everything you say he is, Darling. Before long you will be receiving a little gift to celebrate this wonderful occasion. I'm sorry you live so far away now, for I'd like nothing better than to have one of those cosy talks of which we used to have so many.

Yes, Dear, you may be sure I'll be at your wedding. An atomic bomb couldn't keep me away. Congratulations and a load of good wishes to you and Billy.

Always affectionately,
Aunt Milly

My dear Miss Hillman,

Having known your father for some time, I feel that I want to write you and offer my congratulations on your engagement to Grant Richards. I saw the notice in the *Evening Standard* only last night. It happens that I have the pleasure of knowing Grant, too. We have served together on several businessmen's committees in town.

My very best wishes go to both of you. Please give my kindest regards to your father.

Very sincerely yours,
Bruce Loomis

ON ANNOUNCEMENT OF A MARRIAGE

Dearest Charlotte,

Thank you very, very much for that wonderful letter telling me all about your recent marriage. From all you say, that man of yours must be just about perfect. Or must I make allowance for prejudice on your part? Seriously, I am happier than I can tell you, and I'll always regret that an unkind fate has kept us so far apart that I couldn't be present on the big occasion.

You'll probably not be surprised that I saw it coming. After all, your recent letters contained much between the lines for a friend to read.

My very best wishes to both of you. When you come South, next winter, I want you and that new husband of yours to stay with me for a good visit.

Affectionately,
Emily

Dear Steven,

It was good of you to send me an announcement of your marriage. I received it yesterday, and I want to send my congratulations and best wishes to you and your bride immediately.

Although, I am sorry to say, we did not have the opportunity to become very well acquainted before you left our office, I always felt we had much in common, and I do appreciate this courtesy you have shown me.

Sincerely yours,
Floyd Bergman

Dear Ben,

Three cheers for you! The good news of your marriage has just arrived, and I don't know anything I'd rather hear. You were too fine a chap to be wasted on single life.

When you emphasized how important it was for you to go West, some time ago, I thought your arguments didn't hold water. Being a single man of long standing, I just didn't "get it." But now, I see it all—and you were certainly right. I'll never argue with you again. I'm very glad you have made such good business connections. Your future certainly looks bright from all angles. The only thing I regret is that you are settling down so far away. As you know, I always liked to have you around.

Congratulations to you and your wife, and may there be nothing but the best in store for you both. I'm sending along something for your new home.

Yours always,
Sam

Dear Keith,

That is the best news I have had for a long time. My young nephew married! Congratulations, Boy, to you and your lady.

It was good of you to enclose in your letter the very attractive snapshot of the bride. She is really lovely. Not even all your enthusiasm does her justice. Later on, you must let me have a real photograph of you both—one of your wedding pictures—for your old bachelor uncle to hang in his library.

Well, I won't embarrass you with all those usual remarks about "I can remember you when—" I will say that you have grown into a fine man and I know the girl you have married will be as proud of you as I have always been.

My love and best wishes to you both, in old Alabama, and I hope you and Nancy will use the enclosed check for furnishings for your home.

Affectionately,
Uncle Nat

ON A BIRTH

Dearest Miriam,

Your exciting letter arrived this morning, bringing the happy news that your waiting is over and that you now have two men in the family. I know that both you and Mat wanted a boy, and I was not surprised that he will have his father's name. It's quite a common custom, I know. But I am glad to hear he will not be called Junior.

If I know Mat, he has already selected the college for his son, his daddy's Alma Mater, and probably already sees his boy as another All-American fullback, like his famous father. However that may be, I do know that you both have wonderful dreams for him, and I hope they'll all come true. Your baby is a very lucky little fellow to have you two to love him and bring him up.

Since I cannot travel the many miles between, this letter brings you three my love and the wish that all *your* wishes for your son may come true in full measure, heaped up and running over.

> Affectionately,
> Marjorie

Ruth dear,

How happy I was to receive the good news last night that a baby daughter has arrived and that I am really a great-grandmother! Paul telephoned me from the hospital, which was most considerate of him. He was so much in the clouds and so ecstatic about being a father that I even had to ask him how you were. Not too many men want a daughter for the first child, it seems to me, but there was no doubt in Paul's case, and I know you are happy about it, too.

Congratulations, my dear child, to you both. I have sent you some of those red roses that were your class flower, and I'll be there myself just as soon as your mother assures me that you are ready to entertain visitors. I am so glad the little girl is to have your name.

> Your loving grandmother,
> Lydia Wheeler

Dear Mrs. Quincy,

Since I knew you most pleasantly before you moved away, I want to join those who are congratulating you on the arrival of a little son. I saw the news in our home town paper today. I send you and Mr. Quincy my very best wishes on this happy occasion, and I know that the baby has a fine start in life with such parents.

I understand that next year you may be here, visiting the Brownleys. In that event, it will certainly be a pleasure to see all three of you.

> Cordially yours,
> Natalie Bennett

8

Letters of Condolence and Sympathy, and Replies

Letters of condolence are probably the most difficult of all types that one is called upon to write. Only those who have suffered bereavement themselves can completely understand and sympathize in the loss and grief of another. This does not mean, however, that an acceptable letter of condolence cannot be written by anyone who will apply sincere thought, tact, and understanding to the occasion.

No one can explain exactly how to write such a letter, but the examples that follow may prove helpful with respect to the kind of thoughts to express, and how to express them.

ON DEATH OF HUSBAND OR WIFE

To Acquaintances

My dear Mrs. Norton,

In this evening's paper I have just read the sad news of your husband's passing. I wish to be among those who are offering sincerest sympathy at this time.

One did not have to know Mr. Norton personally to realize how much he will be missed and mourned in the community, for which he did so much.

Very sincerely yours,
Gloria Ward

My dear Mr. Noland,

Please accept my most sincere sympathy in the recent bereavement that you have suffered. Your wife will be long remembered by many. She had a rare warmth of personality and beauty of character that left a lasting impression upon all who met her.

Yours very sincerely,
John Corcoran

To Wife of a Fellow Employee

My dear Mrs. Vincent,

Our office manager told me this morning of your husband's sudden death. I was deeply shocked, and I want you to know that you have my heartfelt sympathy at this trying time. Mr. Vincent and I were associated for some time in our work in the office, and I have lost a very good friend.

Please call on me if there is anything I can do.

Sincerely yours,
Lewis Foster

To Friends

Dear Neal,

The extremely sad news of Lucy's death is something that I can still hardly believe. It is impossible to put into words how I feel, but you know the many things I would say. Above all, I want you to know that, as one of your oldest friends, I am with you in spirit, and only regret that distance makes it impossible for me to be with you in person.

I shall never forget how you stood by me when I suffered the same loss just one year ago, and how you said and did things for me for which I shall be eternally grateful.

My deepest sympathy goes to you in this letter, which is a very weak expression of all that I am thinking.

Sincerely your friend,
Phil

Dearest Lois,

What sad, sad word your letter brought this morning. Your wonderful Norman gone. Words fail at a time like this. If only I could be with you, but you know that I really am, even though there are many miles between. I believe it does help to hear from close friends and to realize that with their thoughts and prayers they are trying to make your heavy burden lighter, even if only a little.

You know what is in my heart, Lois dear. For your own sake I am not writing a longer letter now, but you will be hearing from me again very soon.

Lovingly yours,
Marie

To a Relative

Dear Aunt Libby,

Mother has just written me of Uncle Walt's death, and I know what a blow you have suffered.

Everyone who knew him at all will have lost a real friend, and for all of us in the family he has left a place that can never be filled. I personally shall always feel that way. You know how much he meant to me. I looked on him as a second father, and I think I never knew a kinder, more considerate person.

Please let me know if there is anything that I can do. I could arrange to be away for a week or two at this time and stay with you, if that would be any help. Don't hesitate to call on me.

Affectionately yours,
Ernestine

ON A CHILD'S DEATH

To Acquaintances

My dear Mr. Bendix,

As a neighbor of yours, I want to express to you and your wife my deepest sympathy in the tragic death of your little daughter. She was loved by all who knew her, and I know what a bitter loss you have suffered.

I shall call on you personally a little later. In the meantime, let me know if there is anything I can do.

Sincerely yours,
Jules Corday

My dear Mrs. Haynes,

Mr. Morrow and I offer you and Mr. Haynes our most sincere sympathy in your recent loss

It is, I know, all the harder to bear, since your son had shown such great musical promise. With many others of your friends, we share your sorrow.

Very sincerely yours,
Jeannette Morrow

To Friends

Dear Mildred,

I feel that anything I can say will be futile at this time. When I heard of little Timmy's death, I was so shocked that I could not at first believe it. My sympathy goes to you and your husband from the bottom of my heart.

Sincerely your friend,
Lucy

Dear Lydia and Nick,

Lloyd and I send you our deepest sympathy in your grief over the untimely death of Geraldine. We are sharing your sorrow with you. Having known her so well, we appreciate a little what you are going through, and we stand ready to do anything we possibly can to make your burden perhaps a little easier.

Affectionately,
Grace

Dear Susan and Dick,

We have just heard the very sad and tragic news of your baby's death. It is one of those things impossible to understand, and words are useless at such a time.

We had to let you know, however, that our hearts ache for you both, and that we want to do anything for you that we can. May you be given strength to bear this heavy burden.

Affectionately,
Ada and Bill

ON DEATH OF FATHER OR MOTHER

To a Relative

Dear Cousin Flo,

I was deeply saddened to hear yesterday of the death of your mother. Unfortunately, I was not privileged to know her personally, but I do know that she had a beauty of character and personality that endeared her to all who came in contact with her. My parents have often spoken of her to me.

Nothing can take from you the wealth of wonderful memories, and the happiness that you and your mother shared for so many years.

Affectionately yours,
Margaret

To Friends

Dear Les,

The word of your father's sudden death shocked me severely, and I know well what his passing must mean to you. I realize how close was your association with him for so many years.

I am very glad that I had the pleasure and privilege of knowing him well, for it makes me feel that I can share with you some of the happy memories that will help so much to bring you through these hard days. I know, too, that your faith and courage will bring you peace even in the midst of this great sorrow.

With all my sympathy,
Earl

Dear Josephine,

To think that your mother lived to be ninety-five, and that she passed away so peacefully in her sleep! My childhood associations with her were so close and delightful that I feel unusually close to you at this time.

I remember how she always welcomed me into your home and her unfailing ingenuity in guiding and directing our playtime together. Very vividly I recall the Puritan party she gave for you when you were six years old, and the dolls she dressed in Puritan costume for each of your guests. No child of today enjoys his elaborate birthday affairs as much as we did that simple but clever occasion.

It must be a comfort to you to know that you have cared for her faithfully through these latter years—no daughter was more devoted.

Let me know what plans you are making for the future. I am always interested.

With loving thoughts,
Janice

To Acquaintances

My dear Mr. Graham,

Please accept my most sincere sympathy in the death of your father. I had the privilege of meeting him last month in your office. I shall always remember his delightful personality, and I realize how great is your loss.

The employees in my department join me in this expression.

Sincerely yours,
Wayne Mott

My dear Mrs. Sloane,

As a neighbor, I wish to express my sympathy in your recent bereavement. I know how much it must have meant to you to have had your mother with you during the last few months, and I hope that the memories may make a little easier the sorrow you have to bear.

Very sincerely yours,
Eleanor Sadler

REPLIES TO CONDOLENCE LETTERS

Formal Acknowledgments. (These are often engraved or printed, when it is necessary to answer a large number of notes from those who are not relatives or close friends. For the latter, personal notes are required.)

The family of the late
James Willard Norton
gratefully acknowledge
your expression of sympathy

or

Mrs. James Willard Norton and Family
acknowledge with gratitude
your message of sympathy

or

Mrs. James Willard Norton
wishes to thank you
and to express her appreciation
of your sympathy and kindness

A very brief and formal acknowledgment may be written on a visiting card:

Thank you very sincerely for your note of sympathy.

or

Thank you most sincerely for the beautiful roses.

Informal Acknowledgments

We appreciate sincerely your expression of sympathy and the beautiful peonies that accompanied the note.

or

My husband and I thank you most sincerely for your kindness in thinking of us and for the beautiful chrysanthemums.

My dear Mr. Corcoran,

Thank you very much for your kind note at the time of my recent bereavement. It does make the burden a little lighter to receive such sympathy, and your beautiful tribute to my wife was highly appreciated. It helps a great deal to know that my wife had so many warm friends and that their friendship is mine at such a time as this.

Sincerely yours,
William Noland

Dearest Marie,

You will never know how much your wonderful letter meant to me. Norman's death was so sudden and unexpected that I felt stunned and terribly alone. When I heard from you, it was like having you here with me, and I seemed to feel, in a very real way, your love and strength and support. You are indeed a true friend, and I appreciate all that you mean to me, above all at a time like this.

I cannot write more, now, but I know you understand, Dear. Soon you will hear from me again, and I will let you know all about my plans, which I hope will include a visit with you. It would do me good to be with you.

Affectionately,
Lois

SYMPATHY NOTES ON OCCASIONS
OF ILLNESS OR ACCIDENT

Dear Uncle George,

I was very sorry to hear that you are ill. Please don't misinterpret my saying that it must be pleasant for Aunt Edna to have you around the house and get reacquainted with you. Your business generally monopolizes you, and I know she is enjoying your company. I'm afraid it won't be for long, however, for, as the old saying goes, you can't keep a good man down.

Seriously, I do hope that you will be up and out very soon. No one who knows you, with all your pep and energy, can imagine your being laid low for very long. I wish I were near enough to run in and say Hello.

Affectionately,
Betsy

Dear Ben,

It is too bad that you got in the way of one of those germs that have been taking over the town lately. You are so much on the run, here, there, and everywhere, with that sales work of yours, that I wouldn't have thought any germ could catch you. Don't think for one minute that I am unsympathetic, but the enforced rest may be just what you need to make you let up for a while. You can't do two men's work and not wear yourself out.

Take good care of yourself, Ben, and don't try going back to work too soon. I'll be in to see you when you are feeling a little stronger.

Yours,
Bert

Dear Louise,

I can't tell you how distressed I am to hear of the automobile accident that has put you in the hospital. I am so thankful that you were not more seriously injured. When I hear of what happens to some of my friends who drive cars, I'm glad I don't own one.

Perhaps I'm not striking the bright, happy note for the

patient. You know that I'm sending you all the right kind of thoughts for your early recovery, and I'm coming over soon with some cheerful books that will help you while away the time.

Till then, cheerio!

Mab

Dear Mr. Mahoney,

I am extremely sorry to hear that you are in the hospital with pneumonia. I have delayed writing until I knew you were feeling much better. Your wife has kept me informed as to your progress, and I am happy to know that the report is excellent now.

My whole department joins me in best wishes for your speedy recovery. Relax, now, and get thoroughly well. Don't worry about your work here. We are managing to get along, and your position is waiting for you whenever you are well enough to join us again. I appreciate all the good work you have done for us.

Sincerely yours,
Leonard Babcock

Part Three

TYPES OF BUSINESS LETTERS

9

Letters of Application

A prospective employee may write either of two kinds of letters of application. One is written "cold turkey," as the saying goes—not in answer to a help-wanted advertisement, but to some firm with which the individual has decided he wants to secure employment. The other is the reply to a help-wanted notice inserted by some firm that desires an employee for a particular position.

In both cases, the object is the same, namely, to *sell* oneself and one's ability in relation to the position. Too many applicants emphasize how much it would mean to them to get the job. That is the wrong approach.

The emphasis should be placed on how useful the prospective employee could be to the company. This does *not* mean that he should brag—he should not. He should present *evidence* of previous accomplishment, or, if he is applying for work for the first time, he should give the facts as to the background and preparation that would seem to qualify him.

A long letter is acceptable only if it is entirely to the point—if every statement is needed to sell the applicant's worth to the prospective employer. In your letter, then, include all significant facts, but omit irrelevant remarks and excessive repetition. Put yourself in the busy reader's place. Ask yourself, What information would I want to obtain about an applicant? What details would I expect concerning the applicant's education and experience? Above all, be modest, confident, and completely frank. Never conceal vital facts, for an alert employer will promptly detect the omission of such facts.

The following examples illustrate the basic principles of good letters of application.

INQUIRIES CONCERNING POSSIBLE POSITIONS AND REPLIES TO ADVERTISEMENTS

Number 1

Radford & Phelps, Inc.
100 Fifth Avenue
New York, N. Y.
Gentlemen:
Can you use a young man of good background and education who is capable of performing the following types of work?

1. Proofreading
2. Research
3. Compilation of Statistical Data

Personal Data: Age 34, born in Brooklyn, N. Y., single, no dependents; good health, no physical handicaps; height 5'7", weight 158 lbs.

Education: (1) Graduate of New York University, B.A. degree. (2) Completed several courses at Juilliard School of Music.

Languages: Have studied Latin, Greek, Lithuanian, French, German.

War Record: Served in the U.S. Army, Military Police, Post Exchange Officer, from November, 1942, to October, 1945. Honorably discharged.

Skills and Abilities
1. Can compile statistical data.
2. Accurate and rapid proofreader.
3. Can do market and statistical research.
4. Capable of handling details rapidly and accurately.
5. Familiar with all branches of Music: Theory, Harmony, Counterpoint, Composition.

Present Employment: Am presently employed and have a good record with this concern. I wish to make a change because I am extremely interested in the publishing field.

Salary: Salary is of secondary consideration to the opportunity of a worth-while career.

An interview would permit me to elaborate on my knowledge and experience, and would enable you to determine my suitability to serve your organization.

Yours very truly
Richard Mooney

Number 2

Gentlemen:

Two weeks ago, at the age of seventeen, I graduated from Benson High School, and now I wish to secure a position with a firm like yours. Circumstances make it necessary that I begin contributing to the family income as soon as possible. In whatever position I obtain, I shall work hard and faithfully. I intend to make good, for my family's sake, as well as for my own.

Throughout my high-school course, I maintained an average of 90 per cent, and was among ten students awarded special honors in a class of two hundred. During my junior year, I was Business Manager of the class Year Book, in which capacity I was responsible for the finances. For the first time in three years the book was a financial success. For the last two years of high school I worked three nights a week and Saturdays in our local drugstore, to supplement the family income, and I am working now in a temporary position until I can secure a permanent one. Naturally, I am willing to start in a modest way. I want to learn the business and then go on to better things.

I feel that my school years, with their experience both in and out of school, have helped me to develop qualities that would make me useful to you. I can give you excellent references as to my intelligence and dependability from the principal, from my teachers, and from employers for whom I have worked.

I shall appreciate the opportunity of an interview in order to give you more details in which I think you may be interested.

Very truly yours,
James White

Number 3

Dear Sir:

I am taking the liberty of writing this letter to you, the Editor-in-Chief, because I believe that you personally may be interested in my services.

I am twenty-four years old, unmarried, a graduate of Columbia University, School of Journalism, 1946, rating among the first five of a class numbering one hundred. During my course, I worked for three summers in the Production Department of Rivers and Company, assisting in various capacities and learning methods and techniques in preparation for an editorial career. In my junior and senior years, I was Assistant Editor of the college newspaper, *The Spectator*.

After graduation, I worked three years for the Benson Publishing Company, in the Assistant Editor's office. My work comprised editing manuscripts of many different types, helping in the interviewing of prospective authors, conferring with the Assistant Editor about the acceptance of manuscripts, and doing considerable research and rewriting on some of those that were accepted.

For the last two years, I have been Assistant Editor at Wesley House. In that capacity, I have handled a great deal of the fiction that the firm has published during the past year. Here, again, I have worked with authors, including much consultation and collaboration while they were writing their manuscripts. This procedure saved the firm considerable editorial expense after the manuscripts were accepted for publication.

My relations in my present position are mutually pleasant, but I feel I can use my ability to still better advantage. I believe that my services are worth $100 a week.

I should sincerely appreciate the courtesy of an interview at your convenience. In that event, I shall bring with me the best of references.

Very truly yours,
John M. Starr

Number 4

Gentlemen:

Mrs. Thomas Billingsley, recently connected with your firm has suggested that I write you about my training and ex perience, which she believes might qualify me for the position of secretary in your company. I understand that there will be an opportunity for advancement eventually to a supervisory position.

I am twenty-two years old, a graduate of Norton College, 1949, where I specialized in English Literature and Composition. While in college, I attended night school and studied stenography and typewriting, with the result that during my last two undergraduate years I served, part time, as Secretary to the Dean. I also typed a considerable number of book-length manuscripts for several professors.

For one year after graduation, I studied at the Horton Secretarial School, and during the last three months of that period, at night, I worked with the author, Edith Hemingway, on a manuscript, taking dictation, typing, and even doing some editorial work. I also assisted her with her accounts and her correspondence.

During the past year and a half, I served as Secretary to the Director of the Selwyn Foundation. In that capacity, I took dictation, both personal and by dictaphone machine, handling the Director's correspondence, and attending meetings of the trustees, where I took in shorthand the minutes of these conferences, which I later typed and distributed. I was also in charge of the files in the office and, at the request of the Director, I reorganized them on a more efficient basis. In addition to the duties mentioned, I served as receptionist for two hours of each day for two months, as the Director wished me to learn also that phase of the office work.

I am leaving this position because my family is moving from this location.

For references, I am glad to have you consult the following individuals:

Dean Ella M. Bixley
Norton College
Arlington, Iowa

Professor John O. Hand
English Department
Norton College
Arlington, Iowa

Dr. William Forman, Director
Selwyn Foundation
Philadelphia, Pa.

I shall look forward with pleasure to hearing from you, and I hope to be granted an interview. I feel that my training and experience qualify me to give you the high quality of service which your organization requires of its employees. The matter of salary I should prefer to discuss in an interview.

Very truly yours,
Elizabeth Downing

Photograph enclosed

Number 5

Dear Sir:

In the belief that my qualifications and experience fit me for the position of Assistant Art Director of your advertising agency as outlined in your Want Ad in today's *Clarion*, I enclose a record that makes a long letter unnecessary. You will find that the enclosure tells its own story.

I do, however, desire to call special attention to two points: (1) I have had the variety of experience that you emphasize as one of the requirements for the position that you wish to fill. (2) The reputation of the firms for which I have worked proves that I am capable of meeting high standards.

May I have an interview at your convenience?

Very truly yours,
William D. Dawes

Enclosure

Professional Record of William D. Dawes

My ten years' experience qualifies me to fill the position of Assistant Art Director with taste, speed, and accuracy. The following are highlights, details of which I will gladly furnish if you are interested.

Layouts for direct-mail, magazine, and newspaper advertising, from classified and small space to full page, and from visuals through comps. For three years, I have created seventy-five layouts a month of individual newspaper ads for two national beauty-salon chains, as well as full-page ads in trade and fashion magazines. My present layout work also includes posters, packages, labels, and displays for a line of cosmetics; house organs; promotion material and instruction charts.

As regards *production* of the above-mentioned layouts into completed jobs, I have selected the type, ordered paper, printing, and engravings, directed chain-basis distribution, and done the cost accounting of the whole process. I have made my layouts, dummies, preparation, and production for offset and letterpress, and possess a working knowledge of the other reproduction processes.

My present work must meet the requirements of more than one hundred department stores, and at the same time function on a chain basis. Themes, ideas, and copy interpretations are largely original, but contact men have complimented me on my ability to put their suggestions effectively on paper.

My ten years in this field include working at night as a chartist during my last year at Pratt; creating sales maps and drafting for the Wilson Oil Company; and five years in my present position. Of considerable indirect value have been my copywriting courses at Columbia and the Advertising and Selling course of the Advertising Club of New York.

Number 6

Gentlemen:

In reply to your advertisement in this evening's *Dispatch*, I am applying for the position of typist-supervisor. I believe the following facts show that I could give you services of real value.

I am twenty-one years of age, and graduated in 1949 from the Katharine Gibbs Secretarial School. As you know, the graduates of this institution receive a thorough grounding in business English and good writing, as well as typing and stenography. I specialized, too, in supervisory and executive courses, at the suggestion of my instructors.

In 1950, I was in charge of the typing department of Whitley Brothers, responsible for all their correspondence and also for the supervision of twenty typists. During the year I was there, I increased the production of my department by five per cent and received more salary in recognition of this accomplishment.

For the past year I have held a similar position with J. B

Mosely, Inc. Here I have supervised a department of thirty typists. I was put in charge of a special training class organized to obtain additional efficiency and succeeded in increasing letter production by ten per cent. I have also reorganized and improved the files of the typing department. Mr. Mosely stated that my work was responsible for additional business, and I received another increase in salary.

References:

Mr. J. B. Mosely
14 Somerset Avenue
Hartford, Connecticut

Mr. Robert Whitley
24 Summers Street
Albany, New York

May I have the privilege of a personal interview? I should prefer to leave discussion of salary until that time.

Very truly yours,
Frieda Thomson

FOLLOWING UP APPLICATIONS

Follow-up after a Waiting Interval

My dear Mr. Swenson:

About two months ago, I submitted an application for a position as file clerk in your office. I realize you explained that there were no vacancies at the time, but that you would keep my letter at hand in the event that there might be an opportunity later.

I do not imply, in writing you now, that you would forget me. I just wish to say again that I am certain I could make myself valuable, particularly as, since seeing you, I have taken a special advanced course in filing and have also been working in a temporary position, gaining practical experience.

May I ask whether you can foresee a vacancy in the near future?

Yours truly,
Belle Forsythe

Follow-up of Interview

My dear Mr. Hildebrand:

In accordance with your request during our recent interview, I am submitting in writing some of the data in which you were especially interested.

For three years I was a sales clerk in Halley's Supermarket in Cedar Rapids, where I received an increase in salary and special recognition from the management for my knowledge of the stock and efficient service to customers that helped to increase sales by a substantial percentage.

During the past year, I have held the position of sales and stock clerk at the Self Service Mart, in the same city. Here my duties have included assisting customers in various ways in connection with their marketing problems, as well as helping to place and arrange effective floor and counter displays of merchandise. Here also I was in charge of the stock inventory.

With this knowledge and practical experience of inventory, display, and sales, I feel certain that I can prove myself of real value to you.

I hope to hear from you soon.

> Yours very truly,
> James Bennett

LETTERS FROM COMPANIES ACKNOWLEDGING APPLICATIONS

Dear Sir:

Your letter applying for a position as salesman arrived this morning, and I have read it with more than ordinary interest.

As explained in the advertisement that you answered, we plan to increase our sales staff within the next few weeks. Will you call for an interview on Wednesday, either between 10 and 11 a.m. or between 3 and 5 p.m.? Please ask for me, and bring with you full data on personal background and sales accomplishment.

> Very truly yours,
> Guy Winthrop

My dear Miss Oglethrope:

This will acknowledge your letter of August 4 applying for a position as secretary with our organization.

Your references and your previous record of work are excellent and, although I must be frank and say that there is no opening now, I shall be glad to interview you, if you are willing. There is a possibility that there will be a vacancy within the month.

If I do not hear from you to the contrary, I shall expect you either Thursday or Friday, between 9 and 11 a.m.

Yours very truly,
Arthur Van Slyke

My dear Mr. Corcoran:

Your letter of February 22, in which you apply for a position as bookkeeper, has just come to my attention.

Unfortunately, there is no opportunity at the moment, but I definitely will keep your application in our active files, for I am very well impressed with both your personal and your business qualifications. I suggest that you get in touch with me again in six weeks if you are still interested.

Sincerely yours,
John Stern

REPLIES TO ACKNOWLEDGMENTS OF APPLICATIONS

Gentlemen:

Thank you for your letter acknowledging my application of June 14 for a position as typist with your firm. I note that you say that within a week a temporary place may be open, during the vacation of one of your regular typists.

I shall appreciate your informing me as to the exact time, for I shall be glad to fill the vacancy, in order to prove my ability and in the hope that the temporary assignment may lead to permanent work.

Very truly yours,
Annabelle Hastings

My dear Mr. Barron,

Your courtesy in acknowledging my recent application in regard to the opening for a bookkeeper is much appreciated. I am pleased to hear that within a short time you will need additional assistance and that I may depend upon your letting me know when that time comes.

I feel sure that I can turn my previous experience to good account on your behalf, and I assure you that I will spare no effort to prove my worth.

Sincerely yours,
Alfred E. Dodge

LETTER OF INTRODUCTION

Dear Frank,

Stuart Blake, a young friend of mine, the bearer of this note, will highly appreciate, as I shall, your giving him a few minutes of your busy time.

He would like to talk with you about the possibility of an opening in your copywriting department. In addition to an excellent specialized education, he has already done successful work in copywriting and layout for direct-by-mail advertising. I believe he shows real promise, and I think you will agree with me.

Thank you, Frank, for your courtesy.

Sincerely,
Ed

FOLLOW–UP OF REFERENCES FOR INFORMA–TION ABOUT APPLICANTS, AND REPLIES

My dear Mr. Stokely:

Your name is among several references given by Mr. William Smart, who wishes us to consider him as a possible Office Manager with our firm.

We shall appreciate your giving us your opinion of Mr. Smart's character, personality, intelligence, habits and—very important—his success in his personal relationships with other people. We want a man with originality of ideas and a real capacity for hard work, too. I know that your comments will be valuable, and please make them entirely frank. Anything you have to say will be treated as strictly confidential.

Thank you for your cooperation.

Sincerely yours,
James Todd

My dear Mrs. Wiley:

Miss Josephine Timmons has applied for a position with our organization as receptionist, and has given your name as a reference. We shall appreciate hearing from you.

Of course, you know the importance, to us and to the applicant, of your giving a perfectly frank opinion of her and of the qualifications that she may possess for the job in question. We should particularly like to have your estimate of her personality, her cultural background, and her ability to meet people courteously and graciously.

Strict confidence will be observed concerning what you tell us. Thank you for your assistance.

Yours sincerely,
Thelma Montgomery

My dear Mr. Todd:

I take genuine pleasure in recommending Mr. William Smart as Office Manager in your organization.

For many years I have known him personally, as well as his family, and during his five years in business I have followed his progress with much interest. He is a young man of culture and education, high ideals, and sound integrity. His originality of ideas and capacity for hard work have been outstanding characteristics ever since his high-school days. So far as I am concerned, you may tell him what I have said—I've often told him so myself.

I honestly believe that your firm would be fortunate in obtaining his services.

Sincerely yours,
Alan Stokely

My dear Miss Montgomery:

It gives me real satisfaction to answer your note concerning Miss Josephine Timmons.

She worked in the same office with me for two years as a typist and stenographer and was one of the best-liked girls in the company. Several times she took my place as Secretary to the Office Manager and showed a marked talent for meeting people and for handling problems that arose. Miss Timmons comes of a fine family and is a graduate of Hunter College, where she made an enviable scholastic record. I cannot speak too highly of her.

I am convinced that she would bring credit to you and your organization.

Yours very sincerely,
(Mrs.) Belle Wicks

10

Letters of Inquiry

Letters of inquiry are written to obtain information of one kind or another. The writer (a) may have decided that he wants data on some subject and may communicate with some source from which he believes he can get it, or (b) he may write in response to an advertisement, to learn more than it tells him.

Especially in the first instance, the letter should be very clear and explicit in order that the recipient may know exactly how to comply with the request.

REQUESTS FOR INFORMATION, WITH REPLIES

Number 1

Gentlemen:

I plan to leave New York in three weeks, August 7, and travel by train to San Francisco, taking a rather extended vacation en route. Since I cannot spare the time to do the planning, I shall appreciate the cooperation of your Bureau. Please bear in mind the facts set forth below. Accommodations are to be first-class.

It is my intention to spend four days in Chicago, and I wish to stay near the theater district. From there, I shall go to Denver and stay one week, visiting the principal points of interest in and around the city. If a trip to Pike's Peak from Denver is feasible, I wish to include that. My next stop will be Yellowstone National Park, where a horseback tour of the Park is to be included. After that, the Grand Canyon of Arizona, with the regular sightseeing trip, and Salt Lake City including Great Salt Lake.

Kindly inform me when you have completed the arrangements and I will call at your office to go over them with you.

Very truly yours,

Allen B. Anthony

My dear Mr. Anthony:

This is to acknowledge your letter of July 25, entrusting us with the planning of your vacation trip. Thank you very much for your patronage.

You may rest assured that we will spare no effort to plan a trip which will meet your every requirement, and which will give you the pleasure and recreation that you desire.

As requested, we will inform you when the arrangements are completed, at which time you can call and approve them.

Yours very truly,

Robert Elliott

Number 2

Gentlemen:

Will you please send me information on your grounds service for suburban residences? If it is what I need and want, and is satisfactory as to price, I shall be glad to subscribe to it. I might wish partial, or perhaps complete, service.

I have a ten-room house, situated on two acres of ground. There is a privet hedge extending for some hundred and fifty feet along the front; two flower gardens, approximately 60 by 15 feet, in the rear; and two large lawns to be kept weeded and mowed. There are also a considerable number of shrubs and a grape arbor that require pruning. Will you kindly let me know, too, if your service is year-round, including shoveling of walks and driveways after winter storms?

I shall appreciate hearing from you as soon as possible.

Yours truly,

William Eggleston

My dear Mr. Eggleston:

We thank you for your letter of February 4, inquiring about our grounds service for suburban residences.

Enclosed is a booklet we have prepared especially to answer just such inquiries as yours. You will note that our service varies according to how much the householder wishes to have done. For example, sometimes the gentleman or the lady of the house prefers to care for the flower gardens; and some gentlemen—believe it or not—even like to mow lawns.

Seriously, our service is complete, and all-the-year-round. We keep hedges trimmed; mow lawns periodically and keep them in healthy condition; give flower gardens the best of care and cultivation; take care of all necessary pruning; rake leaves in the fall—and yes, we do keep your walks, driveways, and porches free of snow and ice during the winter.

The enclosed booklet gives you full details, with our rates. May we suggest, however, that you call River 4972 and ask one of our representatives to inspect your property at your convenience. Such a procedure is likely to result in an arrangement most economical and satisfactory to you.

Thank you for your interest, and we shall expect to hear from you again soon.

Yours very truly,
Robert Ames

RESPONSES TO ADVERTISEMENTS

Number 1

Gentlemen:

Please send me by return mail, as advertised in the *Challenge* of March 3, your course on "How to Make Money by Writing." It is understood that this course may be kept and examined for five days and then returned, with no obligation, if I do not wish to keep it.

Very truly yours,
Henry King

Number 2

Box 421
Tribune
Gentlemen:

I am interested in the suburban residence that you are advertising for sale, but I should appreciate a few details in relation to my particular family and present circumstances.

(a) Is there a good shopping and marketing district within walking distance?

(b) Is the immediate neighborhood free from heavy traffic as a menace to small children?

(c) Does the house need any substantial amount of redecoration?

(d) Is there any finished bedroom, with bath, on the third floor?

A prompt reply will be appreciated, as I am seriously considering another house.

Sincerely yours,

(Mrs.) Ethel Bingham

11

Claim and Complaint Letters

Letters of claim and complaint should not be difficult to write. They are based on facts, if there are really good grounds for the claim or complaint, and it is a question of presenting these facts clearly, concisely, and forcefully. One warning is in order: If you want your letter to be effective, you must *know* the facts—not just generalize, jumping to the conclusion that the other fellow is wrong. Sometimes there are the well-known "extenuating circumstances" that make the other side of the case reasonable, too.

CONCERNING DEFECTIVE MERCHANDISE, AND REPLY

Number 1

Dear Sirs:

One week ago, April 2, I ordered fifty lamp shades, my order No. 332, and your invoice No. 920. The shipment arrived yesterday, presumably in fulfilment of my specifications.

The entire lot is unsatisfactory. The color is not as specified; the material is of inferior quality; and the shades are not even all of the same size. Some of them also have defects that are glaringly visible.

I am returning the entire order by express, collect, and shall expect to receive the correct merchandise at your earliest convenience.

Very truly yours,
Arnold Mott

Gentlemen:

Five days ago I was in your house furnishings department and was attracted by your special display of floor linoleums. The clerk showed me several varieties, and one of them, in the size and pattern that I eventually selected, showed wear and several defects in the material.

Naturally, I supposed that this was simply a display item, and it did not occur to me to call the clerk's special attention to the conditions I have described. Imagine my astonishment and disappointment, when my linoleum arrived yesterday, to find that I had apparently received the defective linoleum. I can see no excuse whatever for this whole discreditable business.

I always try to be a reasonable person, and I am willing to listen to an explanation, if you have one. In the meantime, of course, I expect you to send for the defective goods.

Yours truly,

(Miss) Helen Turner

My dear Miss Turner:

Thank you very much for telling us about your unfortunate experience with our house furnishings department. You have done us a favor in bringing this matter promptly to our attention.

The whole affair was inexcusable, so we are not going to try to make excuses, but you will, we believe, be interested in the following rather unusual facts.

The clerk who waited on you had been given his notice of dismissal two weeks before, and the day he waited on you was his last day with our firm. He has admitted that he deliberately sent you the faulty linoleum in order to cause trouble for the firm.

We are, of course, sending immediately for the defective merchandise, and we shall see that your order is filled in a satisfactory manner. In fact, I am giving it my personal attention.

Please accept our apologies for the inconvenience caused you.

Yours very truly,

William Swarthmore

LETTER REGARDING DELAY IN SHIPMENT

Reporting Delay

Gentlemen:

You have generally given us such excellent service that we regret having to call your immediate attention to Purchase Order No. 4721, placed with you, under date of June 14. It should have reached us two days ago, and it still is not here.

Perhaps this shipment is en route now. In any event, we shall appreciate your telephoning us and letting us know exactly how matters stand. If the order is not on its way, please take immediate steps to send it, and mark RUSH. In case you cannot furnish all items now, please ship the men's shaving kits at once.

We shall expect your telephone call upon receipt of this letter.

Yours truly,
Benjamin Caulkins

Acknowledgment of Delay Report

My dear Mr. Caulkins:

This is to confirm our telephone conversation, according to your request. We would willingly take the blame if it were ours, but we have checked thoroughly on the delay in delivery of your order, and have found that everything was promptly and efficiently taken care of at this end. The order was correctly filled, carefully packed, and promptly shipped on June 16, via Trans-State Trucking Service.

We have already reported your complaint to that Service, and a tracer is now out. In the meantime, however, we have made up a duplicate of your order and it is already on its way to you by special truck, at our expense. We fail to understand how this trouble occurred and, as you see, we have done our best to correct matters, for we value you as one of our most highly esteemed customers.

Thank you for letting us know at once about the delay, and we trust that you will receive the duplicate shipment promptly.

Yours very truly,
Carlton Ward

LETTERS REGARDING REFUNDS

Letter Refusing Refund

My dear Miss Whitley:

We have received the blouse that you returned and, with it, your letter requesting credit in full ($8.95) for the merchandise.

It is our aim, as you know, to maintain a generous credit policy, but we are sure you will understand that we have to protect all our customers, and that therefore we cannot accept returned goods that have been worn. Unfortunately, the blouse that you purchased has obviously been worn. Undoubtedly, you simply did not realize the point of view which we have explained.

Since we cannot resell this blouse, we are regretfully unable to credit your account in this instance, even though we certainly value your continued patronage highly and should like to please you.

The blouse is being returned to you by our afternoon delivery. We hope we may serve you in the future.

Yours very truly,
James Ardmore

Letter Granting Refund

My dear Mrs. Montgomery:

In your letter, just received, you call our attention to our guarantee of "Satisfaction or Money Refunded." We note that you have returned the merchandise purchased two days ago, because a mistake was made by one of our clerks and you received the wrong goods. We always live up to our promise to customers and are therefore enclosing a check for the full amount of your purchase.

We really do not make many errors such as this, Mrs. Montgomery, and we take pride in that fact. We value your patronage, so won't you drop in again soon and permit us to see that this time you get exactly what you select?

Sincerely yours,
Morton Powelson

LETTERS REGARDING COMPLAINT AND REDRESS

Letter Regarding Bad Check

My dear Miss Morrello:

I am sorry to have to inform you that your check bearing the date of December 20, drawn to me in the amount of $150 for a used car, is not good.

On December 21, I deposited the check in the Smithtown Trust Company. I received it back this morning with the notation "No Funds." We all make mistakes, at times, in the matter of our bank accounts, and I am sure that this is what happened in your case, perhaps because of heavy purchases for the Christmas season.

Of course, you understand my position in wishing to have the error corrected at once. Will you therefore please send me immediately a certified check for $150 plus protest charge (statement enclosed) which I was required to pay. Your prompt attention will enable me to adjust my account with the bank and to return your original check.

Yours very truly,

James Godfrey

Complaint Regarding Redress or Adjustment

Gentlemen:

Yesterday, owing to your carelessness, I had a very painful accident in front of your building. Serious as it was, my physician informs me that he cannot yet tell what the full consequences will be.

While I was walking along the sidewalk on the south side of 112 Malcolm Street, my heel struck your coal-hole cover, which was not fastened from below, and which flew up to a perpendicular position so that I plunged violently downward, waist-deep, sustaining bruises, abrasions, and severe shock.

My brief case, which I was carrying at the time, was hurled from my hand, scattering valuable original papers in the street, where many of them were damaged so badly that I shall have to go to the expense of having fresh copies made. In fact, one paper, which will require research to duplicate, was carried away by the high wind that was blowing and I never did recover it.

Your carelessness in permitting the condition described to exist was inexcusable. I shall expect to hear from you immediately as to what you intend to do in this matter.

Yours truly,
Robert McIntyre

Company's Reply to Complaint

My dear Mr. McIntyre:

Your letter describing your accident in front of 112 Malcolm Street arrived this afternoon.

We exceedingly regret the fact that you suffered such an experience, and we have already made an investigation on the premises. Recently we have had some trouble with the janitor in regard to certain aspects of safety around the building. He had improved lately, as a result of our careful check upon him, and we had hoped that all was well. This is the only incident of the kind that has ever occurred under our management, and we regret it as much as you do.

Our legal representative will telephone you tomorrow for an appointment to discuss the entire matter. You may rest assured that we wish to arrange a settlement that will be entirely satisfactory to you.

Yours very truly,
Arthur Bisbee

Customer's Letter Threatening Legal Action

Gentlemen:

This matter of the bad paint has reached the point where it would be funny if it were not so serious. Another week has passed since I wrote you my second letter—a total of three weeks since you evidenced such a promising reaction to my original letter of complaint. Still no results.

You certainly cannot possibly think that I have been either unreasonable or impatient. I want action within twenty-four hours or I will place the whole affair in the hands of my attorney.

Yours truly,
Richard Amberg

12

Sales Letters

Sales letters, obviously, are meant to *sell* something. Yet, too often they are stilted and mechanical, lacking in interest to the prospect. A reader will not act unless and until you have made him want what you are trying to sell, and, to do that, you must stimulate his interest.

The time-honored formula cannot be improved: attention, interest, desire, action. It is the function of the beginning and of the end of your letter to get attention and action; the body of the letter must cultivate interest and a real desire for your product or service. But care should be exercised not to write too much "by rule." The sales letter should be natural, sincere, and convincing.

Write while the iron of your imagination is hot—but it is wise to lay your completed work aside and let it cool a bit. Read it, aloud, a little later. If it still sounds effective, send it.

LETTERS SOLICITING NEW ACCOUNTS

Number 1

SPECIAL ALLOWANCE FOR JANUARY PROMOTION OF HOW–TO–DO–IT & SELF–IMPROVEMENT BOOKS!

Are you looking for an easy way to increase your sales? Why not let the EVERYDAY HANDBOOK SERIES do the trick? We feel so strongly about the year-'round sales potential of these popular little books that we will co-operate with you and

offer this series for the month of January with a special allowance for your advertising and promotion.

Certainly you don't have to be told of the perennial demand
for "how-to-do-it" books. The EVERYDAY HANDBOOK
SERIES supplies this demand admirably because it offers practical information for self-improvement in workaday activities
in business, as well as during leisure hours. These up-to-the-
minute digests are on a wide variety of subjects, simplified for
home study. Each handbook is an authoritative yet "popular"
presentation suitable for any reader's permanent reference
library.

Display EVERYDAY HANDBOOK SERIES prominently in
your shop and you will be amazed how fast these books sell.
Your customers will buy them almost as freely as they would
buy magazines, because EVERYDAY HANDBOOKS provide
the alert layman with basic information in convenient form
and at just the right price!

If you would like some of the enclosed EVERYDAY HAND-
BOOK SERIES circulars imprinted for your own use, we
should be pleased to supply them—in proportion to your January stock order. Counter racks are also available—write for
details.

Get your year's business off to a good start with the EVERY-
DAY HANDBOOK SERIES. See the convenient order form enclosed. *Order now to obtain the special allowance.*

	Very truly yours,
Enclosures	BARNES & NOBLE, Inc.

Number 2

My dear Mrs. Whitman:

"The patter of little feet"—that phrase has a very sentimental association, but not where mice are concerned.

If in your home there are little feet pattering about that
don't belong there, call us at once. We get rid of mice, rats,
and other undesirables. Our exterminating service is complete,
effective, reasonably priced, and guaranteed as to results. Our
employees are quiet, courteous, and efficient. They leave no dirt
anywhere. They do not wear uniforms, and our cars carry no
advertising on them.

The exact price of a particular service depends, of course,

on just how much is to be done. We can refer you to many
customers who will recommend both our work and our prices.

Call Wintergreen 210 now, and one of our experts will come
immediately.

Yours very truly,
Lester C. Forsythe

Number 3

My dear Mr. Abercrombie:

Mr. William Best has suggested that we send you some of the
highlights of his latest book, *How to Write What Will Sell*. It
has itself been a best seller in its field ever since publication,
and we are glad to do as he suggests.

The enclosed leaflet you will find fascinating reading, but
it does not begin to be as informative and interesting as the
book. Mr. Best, in this newest publication of his, has gathered
together and made available his many years of experience as
a successful writer of both fiction and nonfiction.

He tells you how to build plots and create lifelike char-
acters, explains how and where to get material for articles of
all kinds, and gives a list of the best markets, with details as
to material wanted and rates of payment.

The book is invaluable both for the person who plans to
make writing a career, and for the individual who would like
to earn extra money through part-time writing.

We want you to *see* this book. If you are not certain that it
is worth to you much more than the moderate price of $3.75,
you may return it, with no obligation.

Don't miss this rare opportunity. Mail the enclosed card
NOW!

Very truly yours,
Charles B. Singer

Number 4

My dear Mr. Vines:

Only a real artist can paint a picture.

Oh, yes, any one can mix colors together, put them down on
canvas, and call the result a picture—but what a difference!

Undoubtedly, you recognize the analogy with respect to letterheads. Some are just letterheads. Others are works of art.

Our pride in being artists in this field is justified by our experience with many well-satisfied customers. We do more than print letterheads. We plan, design, and execute them in such a way that the result does the most credit to your firm. It enhances your reputation and helps to bring in additional business.

Mail us a letterhead of yours now, and we will give you, with no obligation, expert advice as to how we can redesign and print it to make it more effective for your purpose.

Yours truly,
Elite Printers

Number 5

My dear Mr. Atkinson:

You remember the series of cartoons, "What's wrong with this picture?"

Well, how about this one?

You're a bit late waking up, on a cold winter morning. The house seems unusually chilly. You dress hurriedly and rush down to the furnace. You guessed it—the fire needs artificial respiration, and a lot of it. It's dying. You desperately get to work—and you know what happens at a time like this. Everything goes wrong.

You shake the grate, as a terrior shakes a rat—yes, there are a few red coals. So you shovel the ashes and dead coals from under the grate, nicking your hand on the edge of the furnace, and covering your suit and hair with a fine white dust. Now you shovel fresh coal on top of the red embers, open the draft wide, and tear upstairs to clean up, shave, and bolt down some breakfast. Then back downstairs, keeping your fingers crossed. No good. The fire is dead!

Well, you know the rest. Empty the remains, wrestle with coal and kindling, perhaps some of it damp, miss a couple of trains, and finally get to the office an hour or so late, and all out of sorts. And this is a repeat performance—perhaps sometimes with your wife in the uncomfortable starring role, when you are away.

Why keep this up?

Our E-Z Automatic Stoker will solve your problem. Quiet, dependable, it feeds coal to your furnace as needed, and it is equipped with a thermostat so that you can get just the heat you want. And it is simply and quickly installed.

Mail the card enclosed, or telephone Atwater 341, and our representative will call on you at once and inform you of the exact cost of an installation for *you*.

The present moderate prices may have to be raised. Don't delay. Act now.

Yours very truly,
E Z Automatic Stoker, Inc.

Number 6

Dear little Alice,

Welcome to West Haven!

We know you're most welcome of all to your Mommy and Daddy and to your little brother, who arrived only one year ago. What good times you're going to have together! You're going to like West Haven—we're sure of that—and we're sure our lovely town is going to like you.

This letter is to tell you that we have a big store with many pretty things for little girls. There is a special floor set aside for what you may need now, and as you grow older. We have all kinds of nursery equipment—cribs, bathinettes, baby carriages—and dainty wearing apparel for indoors and outdoors. One special item we recommend is our novel snuggle-blanket with zipper, so that you can never get uncovered on a cold winter's night.

Please congratulate your nice parents on your arrival.

Show this "welcome note" to your Mommy and tell her to call us up right away and let us know what you need. We'll have it there before you can say "Baby Bunting."

Your new friends,
Wilson, Merrill & Company

Number 7

Dear Mr. Bellamy:

WE KNOW YOU'RE BUSY—Mr. Bellamy—and that is why we're writing you. It's just because you're busy that we want to save your time when you plan that well-earned vacation trip.

Too often you work so hard, planning, that the actual vacation is not half the fun it should be. You go around from office to office and perhaps write a score of letters, to get assistance. Perhaps some of the letters aren't even answered.

All-Service Travel Bureau saves you that kind of fuss and fret and frustration. As expert professionals in travel, we find, plan, and arrange the trip you want, for what you want to pay. Our facilities, consolidated in one office, cover every phase and kind of travel, and we are authorized representatives of all resorts, tour operators, and transportation companies.

Our advice is free. Our fees are moderate. Our results are highly satisfactory. Our many enthusiastic customers are our best recommendation.

We can help you. Drop in soon, or call Summer 981.

Very truly yours,
All-Service Travel Bureau

Number 8

My dear Mr. Keith:

In your particular work, you are an expert. As such, you know the value of consulting with other experts, in order to benefit from *their* knowledge and suggestions.

Suppose that you had available, at any time, and at a very moderate fee, a group of experts in the field of business, economics, finance, and government, with whom you could consult at any time.

Suppose, too, that each of these experts continually studied and analyzed every authoritative source at his command, and, besides that, traveled both here and abroad to get first-hand information, trends, and reactions.

Then suppose that this remarkable group sent you, every week, a clear, comprehensive, joint report for your personal use and application. You would gladly pay $12.00 a year for their services, wouldn't you?

You get all this in WORLD SURVEY, the new magazine for businessmen, that is on the newsstands this week, for its first appearance. You cannot afford to be without it.

If you act NOW, the enclosed card entitles you to a twenty per cent discount on one year's subscription. This offer is good for a limited time only. Send in the card TODAY!

The Editors
WORLD SURVEY

Number 9

A COLLECTION OF FOLK DANCES
THAT STANDS HEAD AND SHOULDERS
ABOVE ALL OTHERS ON THE MARKET!

FOLK DANCES FOR ALL

Collected and Arranged by Michael Herman, Director,
Community Folk Dance Center, New York City

Even one quick glance at the enclosed page of excerpts from this outstanding book should be enough to give you a good idea of the features which distinguish it:

Clear, yet detailed, instructions for every step of every dance —no bothersome problem of cross references; no symbols or keys to steps to keep referring to.

Line drawings which illustrate difficult steps, formations, and positions—drawings large enough to be seen clearly and understood at a glance.

Exciting, high-speed photographs by Gjon Mili—pictures which impart a spirit beyond the power of the printed word. No postured, out-of-date-looking photographs here!

Background material—without which half of the joy is lost! This is surely no dull recital which gives just the name of the dance and a bare outline of its steps.

Piano scores.

There are many other good qualities, too, as reviewers for such publications as *The Girl Scout Leader, Dance, Recreation, The New York Folklore Quarterly,* and *The Cleveland Plain Dealer,* to name but a few, have pointed out.

With so many outstanding features, you would surely expect FOLK DANCES FOR ALL to cost at least as much as other books of its type. But you are in for a pleasant surprise. The book costs only $1.00, and class orders are billed at your school discount.

If you would like a sample copy of FOLK DANCES FOR ALL, to consider adopting it for use in summer school and fall classes (or at summer camps where you might be a counselor), send us your request on the attached form. A self-addressed envelope is enclosed for your convenience.

Very truly yours,
BARNES & NOBLE, Inc.

P. S. If you would like to see our HOW TO DANCE, ex-cerpts from which are printed on the reverse side of the enclosed sheet, ask for a copy of that also.

SPECIAL LETTERS TO OLD CUSTOMERS

Number 1

Dear Sir:

This is a special letter to you as one of our valued dealer-customers.

Because of the steady pressure of costs, we shall regretfully be obliged to advance by ten per cent our entire line of pen-and-pencil sets, beginning the first of this coming month. Even at some loss to ourselves, we have postponed taking this step until the last possible moment.

Of course, our Sales Department will send you an official notice within a day or two, but we feel that there are certain especially good business friends—you among them—who de-serve preliminary notification like this.

As you know, we do not carry a very large stock, so act now and place your order while you can still benefit from this special opportunity.

Yours truly,
Walter R. Kennedy

Number 2

My dear Miss Horowitz:

This coming month, we are featuring a special sale of ladies' silk dresses of such outstanding value that we want to let you, as one of our good charge customers, know in advance about it.

We invite you to attend a preview of this line, from 10 a.m. to 4 p.m., Wednesday, March 7, the day before it is put on sale to the general public. The dresses to be shown are of exceptionally fine material and design and are offered at attractively low prices, especially considering conditions today. Materials include colorful shantungs, nylons, and silk crepes.

Bring this letter with you to the fifth floor and present it to our Miss Benjamin, who will be glad to give you her personal attention. She will be expecting you.

Cordially yours,

(Mrs.) Amy Benchley

P. S. You may find it a convenience to lunch at our new restaurant just opened on the tenth floor.

Number 3

Dear Customer:

This is our Tenth Anniversary—but *you* are having the party!

After all, that's absolutely appropriate, for it's you, and other good and loyal customers like you, who, by their generous and continual patronage, have made our mail-order business flourish, so that each of our anniversaries has been bigger and better.

All our patrons, old and new, can enjoy the party for the next two weeks. And it will really be a party—with a dozen great bargains for *you* and hundreds of other friends.

The enclosed post cards, which can be used for your orders, give you an idea of what is in store for you. Note, for instance, how we have slashed prices on men's fine handkerchiefs with corded borders and rolled edges; spun nylon socks; three-year-guaranteed stainless-steel cutlery; long-wearing auto-seat covers; and other items.

Look over the enclosed illustrated cards now, and find out what are the articles that *you* want and need. We may not be able to offer you these wonderfully low anniversary prices again —these phenomenal savings for you, your family, your home.

You have a week's trial, *free,* of any starred article you may select. Merchandise is prepaid to your door. If you're not entirely satisfied, return the goods, and owe us nothing.

This opportunity may not occur again. Mail your order cards IMMEDIATELY.

Yours for anniversary savings,

George E. Hastings

Enclosures   President, Buy-Mail Corporation

LETTERS TO REVIVE INACTIVE

Number 1

Gentlemen:

Our business has been excellent lately—many old customers have been generous with their orders; and we have been unusually fortunate in adding a considerable number of new accounts. But we want you to know that not even this state of affairs satisfies us.

We are disturbed about you. Until two months ago, of all our customers you were one of the best, in every sense of the word. Apparently, you have decided to discontinue your patronage. If you were in our place, wouldn't you be puzzled and disappointed?

If you consider us to blame in any way—if there is anything we have done, or have not done, that has alienated you—please let us know and give us a chance to make things right.

Having expanded our premises and added to our staff and our stock, within the last month, we are in a position to give you even better service than before—and we want you to be among those whom we are serving this spring with our full and modern line of household appliances.

Please let us hear from you soon.

Yours very truly,

Gordon B. North

Number 2

My dear Mr. Rinehart:

A while ago, an old friend of mine suddenly just "dropped out"—discontinued his friendly calls, and seemed to want to avoid me when our paths crossed. I don't believe in letting matters rest like that, so I looked him up and asked him, man to man, what was the matter.

It proved that, quite unintentionally, I had hurt him by something I had said—and I immediately cleared up the misunderstanding.

For four months now, you have placed no order with me, whereas we used to have a mutually pleasant and profitable relationship. Am I unconsciously responsible for something said or done that displeased or offended you?

I value your business highly, but even more your good will. So won't you tell me if anything is troubling you that is within my power to adjust? Don't bother to write. Just call me on the phone and let's have a friendly chat.

Cordially yours,
Paul B. Winslow

LETTERS INTRODUCING SALESMEN

Number 1

My dear Mr. Spade:

You have for a long while been a very good customer, and always gave our salesman, Arthur Merriwell, a most hospitable reception. We sincerely regret to inform you that Arthur died suddenly a week ago.

This is a special note to let you know that Richard Fairweather is taking over Arthur's territory, and that he will be calling on you soon. We think a lot of Dick and of his business knowledge and efficiency, and he knows Schwab Hardware from A to Z.

We are sure that you will enjoy with Dick the same friendly and profitable relationship that you knew with Arthur.

Cordially yours,
Carl Beatty

Number 2

Gentlemen:

You will probably regret as much as we do that Bill Hilliard, who represented us so well and for so long, has been obliged to move West for his health. However, Austin Bradley, who for a long while has handled our office work on your orders, is glad of the opportunity to go into the field, and especially glad that you will be among those whom he will serve.

We are sure that our mutually pleasant relations will continue when Austin takes over your area, for we know he will serve you well and that you will like him personally. He will be dropping in on you soon. Thank you again for your many years of loyal patronage. We shall spare no effort to prove worthy of its continuance.

Sincerely yours,
Household Appliance Corporation

13 .

Order Letters

While, at first, order letters might seem to be nothing but purely a routine affair, it is worth noting that they can be made more than that. In other words, whether it is a case of placing an order or acknowledging one, a touch of courtesy and friendliness always helps to form a new business relationship or cement an old one. This principle holds especially true when any misunderstanding is to be cleared up.

Of course, clarity is absolutely essential. It prevents misinterpretation, delay, and sometimes consequent friction and unpleasantness. In all letters concerning orders, then, remember courtesy and clarity. They will go far toward making your order letters a success.

LETTERS ORDERING GOODS

Letter Ordering from a Catalog

Gentlemen:

Please send me by express, collect, the following saws and blades as listed in your most recent catalog:

1 for cordwood and felling	24 A 1328—	2.40
1 for heavy use	24 A 1319—	3.25
1 for pruning and firewood	24 A 1327—	2.15
1 special-duty pruning saw	7 A 823—	1.85
Replacement blades	2 A 1318—	.56
	2 A 1317—	.56
		$10.77

Enclosed is my check for the total amount, $10.77. I shall appreciate your giving this order your prompt attention.

Yours very truly,
Ward Riley

Letter Ordering from an Advertisement

Dear Sirs:

Will you kindly send me two of the portable ice boxes—order number 2 c 321—as advertised in the *Challenge* of yesterday, July 5. Please charge this purchase to my account.

I shall especially appreciate your usual prompt delivery, as I plan to give one of the ice boxes to my daughter, who is leaving on a vacation within three days. One is to be delivered to me at my address, above, and the other to 124 Congdon Street, Apartment 207.

Yours very truly,

(Mrs.) Edith Gross

LETTERS CONFIRMING ORDERS

Number 1

Barnes & Noble, Inc.
105 Fifth Avenue
New York 3, N. Y.

Gentlemen:

This letter will confirm my order, placed by telephone this afternoon with your Mr. Arnold, for the following books of your College Outline Series:

2 Ancient History @ $1.00	2.00
1 Business Law @ $1.50	1.50
3 French Grammar @ $1.25	3.75
1 Latin America in Maps @ $1.25	1.25
1 Spanish Grammar @ $1.25	1.25
Total	$9.75

Enclosed is my check for the full amount ($9.75). Will you please send me these books at the earliest possible moment, as I want to begin using them immediately.

Very truly yours,

Edward Summers

Number 2

Gentlemen:

This letter will confirm my order, given in person to Mr. Charles Boswell yesterday afternoon, for yearly subscriptions to the following magazines:

Everybody's World	$ 2.50
Science for You	3.50
Dental Facts	4.00
The World in Brief	5.00
Total	$15.00

The magazines are to be sent monthly to my office address, given on this letterhead, but please send acknowledgment and bill to:

> Dr. Paul Winslow
> 414 Wedgemore Road
> Addington, Vermont

I trust that there will be no delay in my receiving the order as confirmed in this letter.

> Yours very truly,
> Paul Winslow

LETTERS ACKNOWLEDGING ORDERS

Number 1

My dear Mr. Carol:

We acknowledge with thanks your check and order of November 9 for two extension ladders of the type described in our letter to you of November 2.

It is very unfortunate that the demand has been so great that we have no more of these ladders on hand at present. We regret, too, that we cannot say just when we shall receive a new supply, which was ordered several days ago.

If you wish, we will gladly return your check and will inform you when the new supply arrives. If, however, you prefer, we will keep your check and forward the ladders to you immediately upon their arrival.

> Very truly yours,
> James Allison

Number 2

My dear Mr. Caldwell:

Please accept my personal thanks for your order of March 3. It was a pleasure to receive it and to attend to it myself. The merchandise has already been packed, shipped, and is well on its way. You should receive it within twenty-four hours.

I want to add that, while this is the first order you have placed with us, I trust that there will be many more. Let me assure you that we shall spare no effort to justify the confidence you have shown in us and in our product. We take modest pride in the fact that we have a long list of customers whose first orders were the beginning of a fine business relationship that still continues.

Very truly yours,
William Woodruff

Number 3

My dear Mr. Barnes:

Thank you again, very much, for your purchase of our refrigerator. I did thank you when you gave the order yesterday, at our agency, but I want to express my appreciation once more.

You told me, at the time, that neighbors of yours had recommended us and our merchandise, and that is good to hear, for, after all, people like them are the best possible publicity. But we are not stopping with that. We want you to know that we shall not be satisfied until *you* are satisfied, absolutely, that our refrigerator is really all we say it is.

We stand ready to do any servicing or adjustment, at any time, that may help to give you the 100 per cent efficiency which is associated with our product. It will be a pleasure to serve you.

Yours very truly,
Sidney Baxter

LETTER INQUIRING CONCERNING ORDER

Dear Sir:

Two days ago, we received from you a Newsound portable radio, but there was no letter accompanying it, and none has as yet arrived.

We have referred to our correspondence files, but find nothing from you concerning this matter. In the meantime, our Service and Repair Department has examined your radio and found that the replacement of two tubes is necessary.

We assume that you returned the set for this attention, and we are proceeding accordingly.

You will receive the radio within two days.

Very truly yours,
Roland Seymour

LETTERS REGARDING REMITTANCES

Letter Questioning Report of Payment

Dear Sirs:

We regret troubling you concerning the matter of payment of our bill for the amount of $225.50 (Invoice No. B 347). In your letter of August 2, you state that you had mailed your check, but we have not as yet received it.

Will you please find out whether your bank has cleared it. If it has not, we shall appreciate your sending us a duplicate.

Yours very truly,
James Molloy

Reply to Letter Questioning Payment

Gentlemen:

Your letter concerning failure to receive our check has just arrived.

We are sorry for any trouble you may have been caused. In the meantime, we have stopped payment on previous check (No. 4821) and are enclosing another (No. 4901) for the amount billed ($225.50).

Yours truly,
Henry Burbank

Letter Acknowledging Remittance

My dear Mr. Grauer:

Thank you for your check for $10.50 which accompanied your order of July 7. You should receive the goods within twenty-four hours, as we have already shipped them.

We are taking the liberty of enclosing a special announcement of a discount sale, to be held next month, that we are sending now to a selected list of customers.

Yours very truly,
John Fennimore

14

Collection Letters

Good, successful collection letters are of great importance in business, from two standpoints: (1) they bring in money that might have had to be written off the books, or else collected only through litigation; (2) strange as it may sound, they can actually create good will at the same time that they are persuading debtors to settle delinquent accounts.

But to be successful, the collection letters must show patience, tact, and understanding, often in circumstances that are very trying from the collector's standpoint. At the same time, there must be an underlying firmness, which, in the last resort, is converted into the necessary legal action. Certainly, if the collector follows the preliminary path of patience, forbearance, and tact, the debtor can make no just charge of unfairness if the creditor has to take that final step of litigation.

DIRECT REMINDERS OF ACCOUNTS DUE

Number 1

My dear Mrs. Turner:

Of course, you have many things to remember besides your account with us. We realize that, but one of the things you have forgotten is your check for $38.24, due three months ago.

Since we have our accounts to balance and want to do it without further delay, we are enclosing a stamped, addressed envelope to make it easy for you to send your check by return mail. If this is not possible, will you please inform us when we may expect payment.

Yours very truly,
Walter Stewart

Number 2

My dear Mr. Churchill:

We believe that you are among the considerable number of our customers who not only do not resent a reminder of an overdue account, but who actually appreciate it. There are so many important matters pressing for attention, these days, that it is very easy temporarily to overlook a financial obligation.

You will, we are sure, therefore understand the spirit in which this letter is written and will let us have your check at your early convenience. It may even be that you have already mailed it.

If so, thank you, and just forget this letter.

Sincerely,
George A. Halsey

Number 3

Dear Sir:

Sending out statements and writing our good customers for money is one thing we do not like to do. We like to see your orders. We like to sell you books. We like to give you service—but we don't like the collecting end of the business.

However, it takes money to run a business, and this business is one that depends on turnover—buying and selling. No matter how badly any salesman calling on us wants to sell his product, he has to listen to his credit man for authority and, if we did not pay our bills promptly, we wouldn't be able to have stock for you.

The only reason you are getting this letter is that we believe you have overlooked your account. The amount is $10.45, as shown on the enclosed statement. We hope to receive your check. Thanks.

Very cordially yours,
Radford & Phelphs, Inc.

Number 4

My dear Mr. Wells:

This is a friendly request. It is sent because we believe you have overlooked our invoices of July and August in the amount of $8.06, now just a bit past due.

In view of the possibility that the original invoices were

lost, we are enclosing duplicate copies in order that you may
see exactly what this amount covers. Knowing full well how
busy you are, we send this letter merely as a reminder. We are
enclosing a business reply envelope for your convenience in
emitting.

Thank you in advance for giving this matter your prompt
attention.

                              Cordially yours,
                              Radford & Phelphs, Inc.

Number 5

My dear Mr. Solomon:

Hold it!

Don't file me in that handsome waste basket beside your
desk. It's crowded, and I don't like crowds.

Not under that pile of mail on your desk, either. I couldn't
breathe—and I like to breathe and keep active.

What else do I like?

I like checks, and I like paper clips, and I like *action*. So
just make out a check, fasten it to me with a paper clip, and
mail us, right now, to Good Fairy Company.

                              Always cordially,
                                "A Good Friend"

Number 6

My dear Mr. Ford:

In looking over our records, we find that your account shows
an unpaid balance totaling $67.91.

We are fully aware that a matter like this slips one's mind. It
has happened to us, too. But you must realize that, from our
point of view, it is more serious, and we are sure that you
understand this. According to our check-up, there is no error
in our records, but, if you think there is an error, please let
us know.

It will be highly appreciated if you will pay this balance
promptly or inform us of any reason why you should not do so

                              Yours very truly,
                              William Farrington

Number 7

My dear Mrs. Devoe:

We felt certain that you would give prompt attention to our recent friendly request for immediate settlement of your unpaid balance of $50.98. It is therefore all the more disappointing that you have not given our reminders the attention they surely deserve.

You have generally paid your obligations promptly, and that is why it seems to us that there must be some good reason why, this time, you have for so long left your balance unpaid. To be exact, it is four months since we first billed you. Don't you think that at least a reasonable explanation is due us? This letter is a sincere and friendly request that you settle the account now.

If you do that, an explanation will not be necessary.

Very truly yours,
Ellery Powell

Number 8

My dear Miss Foote:

Maybe you "just forgot"—

Or maybe you overlooked it—

In either event, the result is the same, so far as we are concerned. We are still looking for the $16.25 which is due monthly as your share in the Fowler Development Project, and in accordance with the contract that you signed.

Twice before we have had to request that you meet this obligation, and we fail to understand why. Please write by return mail and explain—or, much better, send a check for the amount in full.

Yours truly,
Allen B. Fowler

SPECIAL APPEALS AND APPROACHES

Appeal to Customer's Pride

My dear Mr. Nelson:

We are going to be frank and tell you something that we believe you would like to know.

We have recently had correspondence with another large

firm, asking us specifically about your credit standing with us. Until very recently, we could have told them that you were among our best and most valued customers in the matter of paying your bills promptly and in full. But now, your May account is still unsettled, after five months, and in spite of several requests from us. You take pride, we are sure, in your business reputation, and we are equally certain that this neglect of yours is a careless oversight. There is still time to remedy the matter if you will send us a remittance by return mail.

In that case, we can still recommend you to the firm in question, for we honestly believe that in the future you will be careful to live up to the excellent reputation that you had established with us.

Yours very truly,
Arthur Moss

Appeal to Customer's Fairness

My dear Mr. Paddock:

If we should happen to meet you on the street and pass the time of day with you, we are certain that you not only would think of that unpaid balance of yours ($47.98), but would mention it.

More than that, we believe that you would give us some good reason why you have not settled your account with us.

You won't think us unfair, we are sure, if we ask you to write a little note, now, and explain why you have neglected this matter—or, better still, enclose a check with your note.

We believe you will agree that we have been fair in this matter—and generally, when that is the case, the other fellow does the same by you.

Now won't you be fair with us?

Very truly yours,
Sun Lamp Company, Inc.

Appeal to Customer's Understanding

Gentlemen:

You know, and we know, that good business is built on mutual understanding—on one person's appreciating the other person's point of view.

We appreciated your point of view three months ago, when we took special pains to attend promptly to your order. Twice we have requested payment, but with no result—not even a reply. You realize, we are sure, that it is prompt remittances that make it possible to continue serving you and other good customers. We are sure, too, that you would have been very much put out if we had neglected your order the way you have neglected payment.

Won't you send us immediately a check for the enclosed duplicate statement?

Yours truly,

Enclosure   William A. Edison

Appeal to Customer's Self-Interest

My dear Mrs. Brandon:

First of all, we want you to know that we consider you a good customer, even though you have owed us payment of $45 for two months now.

Not very many customers realize that it is to their own best interest to pay their bills regularly and promptly, but it is. Therefore it is not just for our own sake that we are urging you to clear this account now. If we are to maintain our standards of quality and fair prices, we must have the cash to pay our own bills promptly, and we cannot do that unless our customers do the same by us. So you see that we have your welfare in mind when we ask you for a check by return mail.

We look forward to your continued patronage.

Yours very truly,

Addison Williams

P.S. The enclosed "preview" of our February sale may interest you.

Letter with Humorous Angle

Dear Sirs:

We had thought of having some mourning stationery printed for writing to people like you, with accounts long overdue. Then we thought better of it, for we didn't want to make you feel as sad about it as we do.

It always makes us feel especially sad when we find new names among our monthly past-due accounts. This month, your name was there, as large as life. There is, however, a bright part to the story—this is the first time you have appeared on the "black list," and we congratulate you on that.

We're sure it was all a mistake—on your part—and that you'll never let it happen again. So just rush a check by return mail, and all will be forgiven.

Cordially yours,
Adam Zabriskie

LETTERS REGARDING A TIME EXTENSION

Request for a Time Extension

Gentlemen:

I am answering promptly your letter of yesterday, urging me to settle my account, now three months overdue, for I want you to know that I am sincere and have no desire to disregard my obligations.

In reply to a similar letter of yours, two weeks ago, I explained that I was having some financial difficulties, and asked that you bear with me a little longer. You know that until recently my credit with you was excellent, and this fact should convince you that I am not now trying to evade my just debts. Certainly such is not the case.

I did not go into details before, because I presumed that my statement about financial troubles would be satisfactory to you. But now let me tell you that within the period in question both my wife and I have been ill, and that my wife's case has required very considerable medical expense and hospitalization. Moreover, since my work is on a straight commission basis, and I was ill for some time, my income was seriously depleted.

Now I am back at work, but I cannot very soon recoup my losses, particularly since my wife is still under a physician's care.

I feel sure that you will understand my explanation, which is given in all good faith and without exaggeration. I should be glad to refer you to our physician for corroboration of my statements. I merely ask that you grant me a little more time and I will fully meet all my obligations.

Yours very truly,
Winthrop D. Heatley

Grant of Time Extension

My dear Mr. Heatley:

We appreciate your letter giving a detailed explanation of your failure for so long to settle your account. If you had written this letter a good many weeks ago, you would have spared both yourself and us a good deal of unnecessary anxiety and unpleasantness.

Sometimes, in cases like this, a customer looks upon a business organization as a mere machine with no sympathy or understanding. If that was your idea, we are going to prove right now that you were wrong. We accept your explanation, and we are sorry to hear about all the illness and expense you and your wife have had to face.

Even in instances like this, however, we do not always make the concession we are going to make to you. But you have had a good record with us and we have faith in your sincerity and integrity. Therefore we are granting you an extension of sixty days from today's date, without even requiring that you sign a note.

We sincerely hope that all will be well with you in the very near future.

Very truly yours,
Robert Southers

SERIES OF COLLECTION LETTERS AND FOLLOW-UPS

Number 1

My dear Mr. Clement:

It may be that our recent request for settlement of your overdue account of $98.45 was mislaid for some reason or other. Generally you have been prompt in your payments.

We shall appreciate your giving this matter your immediate attention. Enclosed is an itemized statement, for your convenience.

Yours very truly,
Robert Nicolls

Enclosure

Number 2

My dear Mr. Clement:

We regret the necessity of again reminding you of your unpaid bill of $98.45, now six months overdue.

In our letter of two weeks ago, we enclosed an itemized statement for you to check. Since we have received no letter taking exception, we assume that the bill is correct.

Kindly send us remittance immediately, or explain any further delay.

Yours truly,
Robert Nicolls

Number 3

My dear Mr. Clement:

In spite of our having recently reminded you twice of your delinquent account with us, we are still willing to assume that your case may be one of overlooking, rather than of disregarding, our requests.

You can easily prove our assumption correct by sending us at once, in the enclosed return envelope, your check for the amount in full that you owe.

Won't you act now?

Yours very truly,
Robert Nicolls

Number 4

My dear Mr. Clement:

It is unpleasant, exasperating, and expensive to continue carrying your long-overdue account on our books, and to have to write letter after letter requesting you to pay the $98.45 that you still owe us. We have not even received the courtesy of a reply.

Therefore we have regretfully reached the conclusion that there is left only the final resort to legal measures, and we have placed your case in the hands of our attorney.

Yours very truly,
Robert Nicolls

Letter from Attorney to Customer

My dear Mr. Clement:

This morning I received from Mr. Robert Nicolls full information regarding your delinquent account with his firm, together with a letter authorizing me to collect the amount ($98.45) now long overdue.

You have neither denied the claim nor given Mr. Nicolls any explanation of your failure to meet your obligation. Therefore, I hereby notify you that, unless I hear from you within three days, I will institute legal proceedings for the collection of the sum herein mentioned.

Very truly yours,
Arthur B. Vandeventer
Attorney-at-Law

Letter from Customer to Attorney

My dear Mr. Vandeventer:

I have your letter threatening legal action to collect my overdue account of $98.45 with Mr. Nicolls' firm.

There is no question as to the claim. Moreover, I have doubtless been very foolish to disregard Mr. Nicolls' numerous communications, but I have had the perhaps mistaken idea that, in the circumstances, nothing would have been gained by writing.

Now, however, let me explain that, within the period in question, my business failed and I have had an extremely difficult time settling my affairs, and also forming a new connection. This I have finally succeeded in doing, and the outlook is good.

Tomorrow I will drop in at your o
will make payment of at least one-third of the amount I owe. The balance I believe I can settle in the near future.

I trust that this arrangement will be satisfactory to you and Mr. Nicolls, and I am sorry for the inconvenience that I have caused.

Sincerely yours,
Ward B. Clement

15

Credit Letters

Too often the underlying meaning of the word *credit* is forgotten. Derived from the Latin, it means "faith," or "confidence." Credit is the foundation of business on the highest plane. Those who write credit letters would do well to remember the fundamental meaning of the word. The person who requests credit should expect to furnish a basis for confidence upon which the creditor can establish a satisfactory relationship.

The credit man should write letters that are dignified, straightforward, sincere—letters that make it clear that the interests of the prospective customer and of the firm are the same. Even a letter refusing credit, or suspending it, if skilfully written, can carry with it a spirit of good will that may yet be the means of establishing a mutually successful and pleasant business relationship.

REQUESTS FOR CREDIT

An Order Accompanied by Request for Credit

Dear Sirs:

I should like to order two dozen pairs of your men's shoes No. 4621 A, at $7.45 a pair, as listed in your April catalog.

Also, I request that you open an account for me with the order listed above. The following references will furnish, I am sure, all the desired information and recommendations as to my business standing that you may require:

> Brown, Carroll & Co.
> 48 Vine Street
> Springvale, Ohio

Saunders & Emory
Springvale, Ohio

Springvale Chamber of Commerce
Springvale, Ohio

As I wish to push my spring business, I shall sincerely appreciate your establishing my credit account at your earliest possible convenience.

Yours truly,
Willard D. Gallagher

Request for Opening of Account

Gentlemen:

This is to request that I be allowed to open a credit account with your organization.

No doubt, you will recall that I have been buying auto parts from you for some time now, on a C.O.D. basis, but I should like the decided convenience of charging my purchases. What I want is an arrangement whereby I can pay my bills within thirty days from the date I receive my invoice.

My business has grown materially during the past year, and I have recently added to my lists such substantial customers as Swiftway Trucking Company, Morrison Storage & Van Company, and the Hillcrest Garage and Servicing Chain.

I have my account in Hillcrest Bank and Trust Company and gladly refer you to their Vice-President, Mr. Willard McIntosh. Other references who will vouch for my personal and business integrity and reliability are:

Wentworth Auto Supply Corporation
Branford, Vt.

Ainsley & Son
Southview, Mass.

Powers & Ames
Hillcrest, Maine

I am certain that the references given herewith will prove entirely satisfactory, and I therefore hope to hear favorably from you in the very near future.

Yours truly,
Ellsworth Morrow

INQUIRIES REGARDING CREDIT STANDING AND REPLIES

Number 1

Gentlemen:

William A. Arnold, Inc., recently gave us your name as a reference when they applied for a credit account with us.

Will you kindly furnish us with all pertinent information regarding the firm in question, particularly as regards the promptness and regularity with which they meet their financial obligations. Of course, anything you tell us will be treated entirely confidentially.

As we should like to inform the Arnold Company at the earliest opportunity, we shall sincerely appreciate hearing from you soon. We shall be glad to do you a similar favor at any time.

Yours very truly,
Lyman Fiske

Number 2

My dear Mr. Lovejoy:

We have received from Mr. James A. Gable, of 4? Cowan Boulevard, Symington, New York, a request that we grant him a line of credit, and your name is among the references that he has given.

It will be highly appreciated if you will send us, in the enclosed return envelope, a perfectly frank statement concerning his dealings with you, and your opinion as to his character, integrity, and financial dependability.

You may be sure that this report will be treated as strictly confidential. Thank you for your valuable cooperation.

Very truly yours,
Herman S. Willkie

Reply to Number 1

My dear Mr. Fiske:

As requested, we are replying with perfect frankness to your recent letter of inquiry regarding William A. Arnold, Inc., as a credit risk.

We regret having to tell you that, in all fairness to you, we cannot recommend the firm. Although for six months we did grant them generous credit privileges, they proved remiss in their payments and disregarded our appeals that they meet their obligations as agreed. Consequently, we were obliged to withdraw those privileges and do business with them only on a strictly cash basis.

That is the only basis we consider safe for dealing with the firm in question.

Yours truly,
Arthur Mayhew

Reply to Number 2

My dear Mr. Willkie:

It is a pleasure to answer your letter asking about Mr. James A. Gable.

We have dealt with Mr. Gable for four years—on a credit basis all that time—and consider ourselves fortunate to have him as a customer. He has never had a post-due account. Not only that, but he has sent us quite a few customers equally reliable. Evidently, to judge from his purchases, he is a man of considerable means.

We recommend him to you with no reservations.

Yours very truly,
Frederick B. Lovejoy

REPLIES TO CUSTOMERS WHO HAVE REQUESTED CREDIT

Letter Granting Credit

My dear Miss Ward:

Thank you for the expression of confidence and good will which your request for a charge account implies.

The references you submitted have been checked, and we compliment you on the high esteem in which you are held by those with whom you deal. An account has been opened for you, and we trust that you will make use of it soon, and often. You will find ordering by telephone a convenience, and such orders will receive prompt and courteous attention.

We send out statements the last of each month, and we

shall appreciate payment sometime within the month immediately following.

Advance notice of special sales and other features of interest will be sent you as a credit customer, and we shall spare no effort to make all your dealings with us pleasant and satisfactory.

Yours very truly,
James Ettinger

Letter Refusing Credit

Gentlemen:

First of all, thank you for your large order for Pure-Air Ventilators, which you placed with our Mr. Thatcher on March 4, and your request that we open a credit account for your firm.

We are sure you understand that, before we authorize such an account, we try to get all possible information that might justify our granting a line of credit. This we have done in your case. Please do not misunderstand, but, on the basis of facts and figures so far secured, we have not been able to make a definite decision to grant you the credit requested.

In view of the circumstances, we do not at present feel quite justified in opening an account for you. If you think that our decision is unwarranted, or if you can furnish us with information that we now lack, do not hesitate to write us or call personally at our office. We should be most happy to reach a better understanding.

It may well be that circumstances may change and that we might then be able to accede to your request. In the meantime, we do value your patronage and shall be happy to serve you, as before, on a C.O.D. basis.

Very truly yours,
William T. Ainslee

Letter Notifying of Credit Suspension

Dear Sirs:

We wish to thank you for your generous order received yesterday, which you ask us to ship immediately and charge to your account.

Your order is already being assembled. However, you

probably have overlooked the fact that for some months you have allowed your account to go unsettled. Since it is our policy to suspend credit until all past-due bills are paid, we request that you send us immediate remittance for the statement already twice rendered. You will understand that no discrimination against you is intended or implied.

Our only wish is to serve you promptly and we will ship your order immediately upon receipt of your check.

Yours very truly,
Richard Hammond

16

Letters to Government Officials

It has been well said that democratic government is just as good as the people really want it to be. There is no better way to take part in your government than to keep your elected representatives informed of how you feel and what you want, regarding current issues and affairs.

Then, too, there are innumerable kinds of valuable information and co-operation which the government offers to the individual citizen. It pays to know how to go about asking for what you would like.

The letters that follow will, it is hoped, prove helpful in illustrating how letters of this type can be written effectively.

LETTER REQUESTING A PUBLICATION

Dear Sir:

I understand that every year your Department of Education publishes and has available, for free distribution, upon request, a bulletin consisting of a list of the Masters' and Doctors' theses, written by students at universities throughout the country, on the subject of education.

As an editor, I am very much interested in the possibility of contacting the authors of such publications, with a view to perhaps giving them professional assistance in additional writing that they may do. I presume that subjects treated include current educational conditions in the United States, federal aid to education, and democracy in education, in all of which I have made some specialization.

Can you tell me whether any of the studies that you list are available for consultation in public and institutional libraries?

Thank you for your co-operation. I shall appreciate receiving the material at your early convenience.

Very truly yours,
Leslie Downes

LETTER TO A SENATOR

My dear Senator:

I note that the House is at this time discussing a bill designed to tighten and enforce restriction of the entry of undesirable aliens into our country. I have already written my Representative urging passage of this bill, and am now appealing to you, in the event the legislation goes to the Senate.

With many other loyal American citizens, I am gravely disturbed regarding the apparent unconcern of our government over the fact that visas have recently been issued permitting entry to not a few aliens who are not only undesirable, but actually dangerous, particularly under the present international conditions. More and more will come just as long as our government continues to pursue a policy that is little short of criminal.

It is high time that we realize that we are at war, whatever euphonious term some may employ, and that we act accordingly with respect to a human menace that can do irreparable harm if it is not quickly and effectively checked.

Will you kindly let me have your views on this matter?

Very truly yours,
Lemuel Wilson

LETTER TO A REPRESENTATIVE

My dear Sir:

I am asking you as my Representative to take any necessary and appropriate steps to restore an adequate and efficient delivery of the United States mails.

Since the service was curtailed, by what many Congressmen, as well as ordinary citizens, considered very abrupt and shortsighted action, the service has been highly unsatisfactory. Deliveries have been slow, late, and undependable, and the postal employees have been rushed and overworked because of the shortage of assistance caused by the dismissal of a large number at the time the bill was passed reducing postal service.

There are many better ways in which government economy can be practiced—ways that have not even been tried as yet. If only a few of the many channels through which the government is wasting the taxpayers' hard-earned money were eliminated, there would be plenty of money for our former good postal service and a lot more things that are needed.

I shall appreciate hearing from you in the immediate future, for I want no doubt in my mind as to how you stand on this matter.

Very truly yours,
Millard Logan

17
Good-Will Letters

Most business letters can, and should, be good-will letters —yes, even those dealing with collection and refusal of credit. It is the spirit, not the subject matter, that counts.

But the correspondence in this section is designed to illustrate the type written *primarily* to build good will, without which no business can long exist. This kind should be relatively informal and entirely sincere. It *should not* indicate or imply that it is a lure to get or keep customers. It *should* reflect a genuine friendliness that will prove to the recipient that not all dealings are "strictly business." Such letters pay generous dividends.

The following examples illustrate sound underlying principles.

WELCOME TO A NEW CUSTOMER

My dear Miss Ray:

This is a friendly note of welcome as you become a depositor in The People's Bank.

Too often business is done on a purely formal and impersonal basis, but we don't subscribe to that policy. We try to live up to the title of our institution, and we want you to think of us not merely as cashiers, tellers, and bank officials, but as friends of yours—all of us—who stand ready to serve you in every possible way.

We shall be happy to give you the benefit of our long and thorough experience in financial matters, at any time, and we feel sure this is the beginning of a long and pleasant relationship.

Cordially yours,
William O. Cornell
President

KEEPING THE PRODUCT SOLD

My dear Mr. Waite:

Three weeks ago, we sold you one of our Welbilt power lawn mowers, and we feel sure that it is proving to be all that it is claimed to be.

But we should be very glad to hear from you anyway, because it is always a pleasure to receive word from customers who are entirely satisfied with our products. Indeed, that is the biggest satisfaction in business.

We want to emphasize again that we shall be happy to make any adjustments of the machine, at any time, that will insure its operation at top performance.

Thank you again for your patronage.

Sincerely yours,
Donald Blaine

APPROACHING A PROSPECTIVE CUSTOMER

My dear Mrs. Wainwright:

May we bid you a sincere welcome as a new resident of Great Falls?

We are certain that you are going to like this community, and that you will find the business people just as much friends of yours as the neighbors who live on your block.

When you are downtown, shopping, won't you make Easton's Restaurant a regular stopping place for luncheon? You will find here not only delicious food at moderate prices, but quick, efficient service and a restful, homey atmosphere that will make every call a real pleasure.

I shall look forward to welcoming you personally, and soon, I hope.

Cordially yours,
Charles Boal
Manager

CHRISTMAS GREETING

My dear Mr. Collingwell:

It is good, at least once a year, to lay aside business formalities and to write a letter purely in the spirit of the season.

You have long been a very good customer, but, more than that, you are also a very good friend. and I want you to know that I truly value that relationship. If you never gave me another order, I would still want you as a friend. I just wouldn't feel right if you weren't dropping in every little while.

So here are my warmest and most sincere Christmas greetings to you and yours. May all the true happiness of the day be yours, and may it continue with you throughout the coming year.

Cordially yours,
Anton B. Drew

Part Four

SOCIAL AND BUSINESS
TELEGRAMS

REVISED RATE SCHEDULE for WESTERN UNION DOMESTIC TELEGRAMS

(*Note:* You now get 15 words instead of 10 to start with in Telegrams—50 words instead of 25 to start with in Night Letters. In many cases Money Order charges have also been made correspondingly lower. The rates shown may be changed from time to time. For current rates and full details communicate with your nearest Western Union office.)

Mileage Zones	Where the Telegram Rate Is:		The Night Letter Rate Is:		The Day Letter Rate Is:	
	For 15 Words or Less	*For Each Additional Word*	*For 50 Words or Less*	*For Each Additional 5 Words or Less Over 50 Words*	*For 50 Words or Less*	*For Each Additional 5 Words or Less Over 50 Words*
0–125	$1.20	6.0¢	$1.05	8.0¢	$1.75	13.0¢
126–225	1.30	6.5	1.10	8.0	1.85	13.5
226–425	1.45	7.0	1.25	9.0	2.10	15.5
426–750	1.60	8.0	1.40	10.5	2.30	17.0
751–1125	1.75	8.5	1.50	11.0	2.50	18.5
1126–1550	1.90	9.5	1.65	12.0	2.75	20.5
1551–3000	2.10	10.5	1.80	13.5	3.00	22.0

18

Information Concerning Telegrams

TELEGRAMS ARE ideal for sending messages on special occasions, such as birthdays, holidays, weddings, and anniversaries. They are also highly effective in business communication, as in acknowledging orders or inquiries, expediting transactions, and providing salesmen and customers quickly with up-to-date information.

The following discussion, adapted from Western Union publications, presents many useful suggestions.[1] Additional information and assistance may be secured from the nearest Western Union office.

TYPES OF TELEGRAMS

Fast Telegram. Receives precedence over all other traffic. Accepted any time of day or night for immediate delivery. Starting allowance is 15 words.

Day Letter. May be sent any time. A deferred service; it will reach its destination in an hour.

Night Letter. Economical overnight service accepted any time up to 2 A.M. for delivery the following morning. Excellent for business messages and for social correspondence of all kinds. Words cost only a few cents. Starting allowance is 50 words.

[1] The material in Part Four of this book has been taken largely from "The New Western Union Telegrammar," with permission of the Western Union Telegraph Company. See also "Your Western Union Teledater" and the leaflet, "Social Telegrams."

Money by Telegraph. The quickest way to send or summon cash safely from one place to another. Just call at your nearest Western Union office, deposit money and it will be telegraphed immediately to its destination. Overnight money orders are accepted any time up to 2 A.M. for certain payment the next morning. Money orders by telegraph are ideal gifts which can be used for cash or purchases.

BIG TRIFLES ABOUT TELEGRAMS

Full Name and Address. There is no charge for the full name and address of the person you are telegraphing, so write out in full to insure prompt delivery. Spell such words as *north* and *south*. Do not use suffixes for street numerals (write "80 North 34 St." instead of "80 N. 34th St."). Give apartment number or floor when known.

Identification. If you do not know the address of the person you are telegraphing, identify him in some way— e.g., "John Jones, Garage Owner." You may also add one identifying title to your signature, without charge—e.g., "George Stewart, Manager."

Figures. Often, figures are easier to read than words. Each group of 5 numerals or less is counted as one word. The figure 2, by itself, is one word; the group 24738 is also charged as one word.

Your Own Name and Address. Give this information so that Western Union will be able to get in touch with you if necessary. If you expect a reply and are not sure the addressee has them, include your own name and address in your telegram.

Punctuation. There is no charge for punctuation marks of any kind, and you can use as many as necessary.

PHONETIC CODE

To make sure that you give or take a telegram correctly over the telephone, you may use, if you wish, the following phonetic code to clarify letters of the alphabet.

A as in ADAMS   N as in NEW YORK
B as in BOSTON   O as in OCEAN
C as in CHICAGO   P as in PETER
D as in DENVER   Q as in QUEEN
E as in EDWARD   R as in ROBERT
F as in FRANK   S as in SUGAR
G as in GEORGE   T as in THOMAS
H as in HENRY   U as in UNION
I as in IDA   V as in VICTORY
J as in JOHN   W as in WILLIAM
K as in KING   X as in X–RAY
L as in LINCOLN   Y as in YOUNG
M as in MARY   Z as in ZERO

INTERNATIONAL TELEGRAPH SERVICE

Full-Rate Cablegram (FR).   Full Rate messages may be written in any language that can be expressed in Roman letters, or in secret language. A minimum charge for 5 words applies.

Cable Letter (LT).   An inexpensive overnight service for plain language messages. A minimum charge for 22 words applies, one-half full rate.

International Money Order.   Deposit money at nearest Western Union office and the money will be sent abroad. Total charge consists of small percentage of amount sent plus full-rate charge for each word of money order message and any accompanying personal message.

Shore-Ship.   In association with connecting radio-telegraph companies, Western Union provides rapid communication to and from ships at sea in all parts of the world.

19

Model Telegrams

THE FOLLOWING models (from "Social Telegrams," published by the Western Union Telegraph Company) provide a handy reference of suggested sentiments for many occasions. They may be used conveniently with variations, adaptations, and additions to fit the individual's needs.

ANNIVERSARIES

Best wishes and love to you on your anniversary.

Congratulations on your anniversary. May each new one bring added joys.

May your anniversary be filled with joy; may you be surrounded by loving friends, and live to see many more such celebrations.

Much love to you both today on your wedding anniversary.

Congratulations. May this anniversary lead to a golden one with golden years between.

Our heartiest congratulations on your wedding anniversary.

Congratulations. May you have many more happy anniversaries.

Anniversary greetings to one who has shared the years with me.

BIRTHDAYS

The best of everything to you, today and always.

Many happy returns of the day.

Love and best wishes for a happy birthday.

Congratulations and sincere good wishes on your birthday.

Wishing you health and happiness on your birthday and for many years to come.

No way I know can be quick as this for sending my love and a birthday kiss.

Love and greetings to the best mother (dad) in the world on her (his) birthday.

Hope that this gift will add in some small measure to all the joy and happiness I wish you on your birthday.

BIRTHS

Congratulations to both of you and happiness and health to the new arrival.

Love and good wishes to baby and mother. Know you are happy to welcome another.

Congratulations. Thrilled and happy to hear the good news. May the newcomer be a pride and joy to you always.

Wanted you to be among the first to know. Just arrived ... pounds ... ounces girl (boy). Mother and daughter (son) doing fine.

Thrilled and happy to hear the good news. Here's just a small token of welcome for the new arrival.

BON VOYAGE

Bon Voyage and the happiest journey to you.

Sincere good wishes for a safe and happy crossing. May good luck and success be your shipmates.

Bon Voyage. Pleasant time and safe return.

Love and all good wishes for a safe and delightful voyage.

CHRISTMAS

All my love on Christmas to those whose love has always meant so much to me.

May Bethlehem's message of peace and happiness be yours today and always.

Happy holiday, and may the $25 with this telegram make it even merrier.

The largest of stockings would never do to hold all my wishes this Christmas for you.

COMMENCEMENTS

May your graduation day be the commencement of a continued series of upward steps to success.

So proud of you and confident you will do even better in the great school of life.

Best wishes and congratulations on your graduation. May the road ahead be one of health, happiness and great accomplishment.

Cheers and congratulations for a good finish.

To a clever miss, on her graduation, go a special kiss and congratulation.

We wish we could be present to see you graduate. But this Gift Order comes with our love for some remembrance of your own selection. Good luck.

COMMUNION

May the blessings of this first Holy Communion day be with you all through the years.

Your first Holy Communion is a great milestone in your spiritual life. Blessings and good wishes.

CONDOLENCES

My (Our) heartfelt sympathy in your great sorrow.

We are grieved beyond expression to learn of your loss. God bless you and comfort you.

I (We) share your loss and send you my (our) deepest sympathy.

In your affliction may the knowledge that your friends share your sorrow be a solace to you.

My (Our) deepest sympathy in your great loss. If there is anything I (we) can do, do not hesitate to let me (us) know.

CONFIRMATION

May the blessings of this Holy Confirmation day be multiplied throughout the years.

On this blessed Confirmation day we pray God's grace for you for many years.

CONGRATULATIONS

On Promotion

Happy to hear of your promotion. Hope it is just one of many more. Sincere congratulations.

Hearty congratulations on your promotion. No one could deserve it more. Good luck and the best of everything.

On Election to Office

Congratulations. The best man won.

You fully deserve the honor. Congratulations and good luck.

Success of Artist

Tremendously thrilled by your great performance.

I have never been so moved by a performance. You were magnificent.

Congratulations and best wishes for continued success.

On Opening New Store

I wish you a prosperous future and all good luck with your new store.

With all good wishes for your grand opening and a success for your new store that exceeds all your expectations.

On Making Speech

Congratulations on your great speech. It was a masterly presentation of the facts.

Your speech was outstanding. It expressed the sentiments of right thinking people everywhere.

Public Service

Congratulations to a real public servant. You have rendered a great service.

Congratulations on a great and courageous job. True Americans everywhere will be proud of your accomplishment.

On Winning Prizes, Awards, Etc.

Congratulations on winning the . . . prize. You richly deserve the high honor.

Just heard the great news. Hats off and congratulations to a deserving winner. If you need any help spending it, just telegraph collect.

CONVALESCENCE

Sorry to hear of your illness. Best wishes for a speedy recovery.

I am sending this wire instead of a letter, to tell you to hurry up, get better.

Best wishes for a speedy recovery and all the luck in the world.

I heard you were ill; it made me feel blue. As soon as you're better, I'll feel better, too.

EASTER GREETINGS

Lots of good wishes for Easter, plus many, many more for the rest of the year.

May the beauty, joy and holiness of the wonderful Easter season abide with you throughout the year.

ENGAGEMENTS

Delighted to hear the good news and wish you great happiness.

May your engagement be filled with a joy only exceeded by the happiness of your married life.

Thrilled with the news of your engagement. Let this Gift Order with my love contribute something to your hope chest.

FATHER'S DAY

Love and best wishes to the finest dad in the world on your day and every day.

Greetings on your day to the finest dad a fellow (girl) ever had.

INVITATIONS

Having class reunion at the old school. We're looking forward to seeing you again.

Extending cordial invitation to hear talk on modern home decoration Women's Club Friday at three. Refreshments.

To my (our) ... party you're invited. If you can come I'll (we'll) be delighted. R.S.V.P.

MOTHER'S DAY

All my love to the dearest mother in the world.

Of all life's treasures, your love and guidance have been most precious to me. All my love.

Love and kisses to the dearest mother of them all, not only on Mother's Day but every other day as well.

NEW YEAR GREETINGS

Best wishes for a happy and prosperous New Year. May the joy of this season remain with you all year 'round.

May the New Year bring you and yours a full measure of health, happiness and prosperity.

May God's grace make each day of the New Year bright for you and yours.

"THANK YOU" SENTIMENTS

Thanks for a lovely evening. We had a grand time.

Thank you for your lovely gift. It was a delightful surprise.

Thank you for your good wishes. I was very glad to get them.

THANKSGIVING

Best wishes for a very happy Thanksgiving.

Best wishes on this end of the wishbone—long or short—for a happy Thanksgiving to you and yours.

Wish I (we) could be home today for that wonderful Thanksgiving dinner and a share in the other festivities. Best love.

VALENTINE GREETINGS

Love may be the last word in some telegrams but it's the first and most important in this one.

This is sent in your direction with all my love and my affection.

All my love to my husband (wife) who is the dearest of Valentines to me today and always.

WEDDINGS

Heartiest congratulations and all best wishes. May all your days be as happy as this one.

Congratulations to the groom, best wishes to the bride. Through all the years a happy life and lots of luck besides.

Congratulations and best wishes for a long life, prosperity, health and happiness.

Love and best wishes to you both. May you always have fair weather and clear sailing.

My sincerest wishes for a long and happy life. Please use this Gift Order in any way that will add to your happiness.

Index

187